FULLER
OF SUSSEX

A GEORGIAN SQUIRE

GEOFF HUTCHINSON

For my grandson
ELLIOT
This is the past
The future is yours

First published 1993

Copyright © G Hutchinson

All rights reserved. No part of this book may be reproduced or transmitted in any form or by any means, electronic or mechanical, including photocopying, recording or on any information storage and retrieval system, without prior permission from the author.

ISBN 0 9519936 0 7

Design, artwork and typesetting by the author
Photography by the author unless otherwise stated
Text set in 10/11½pt Century Book
Printed by M & W Morgan, Red Lake Terrace, Ore, Hastings

Contents

4 Foreword
5 Preface
7 The time
13 The place
17 The squire
21 Builders of fortune
29 Son of a preacher
33 Politics: The first steps
39 The gentleman soldier
43 Romance and rejection
49 Unexploited wealth
51 To serve for Sussex
55 A bitter contest
65 Misguided loyalty
71 Disgrace
77 1812 overtures
79 A Georgian Pharaoh
81 Paint me fine pictures
85 In search of improvements
91 Violation of privacy
93 Beyond the call of duty
99 A friend to science
103 For those in peril
107 Today I buy a castle
113 The paths of glory . . .
125 Legacy: The buildings and follies
146 The final word
151 Chronology of events during Fuller's life
152 Acknowledgements/Picture credits

Inside back cover
    The Folly Trail

Foreword

Having lived in Brightling some 50 years I have naturally absorbed much of the history and legends surrounding the place.

Geoff Hutchinson has ranged far and wide in his research into the Fullers of Brightling and in particular the personality of Jack Fuller, the most celebrated member of the family, which owned and developed the estate over some 200 years.

I think I can say that Geoff has left no stone unturned in his search for information regarding the life and interests of Jack Fuller. As a result he has written a fulsome account of Fuller's life and times and I commend his perseverance to anyone interested in this remarkable man.

Mrs Rosemary Grissell
Brightling
East Sussex

Other titles by the same author:
THE MARY STANFORD DISASTER — The story of a lifeboat, November 15th, 1928
GREY OWL — The incredible story of Archie Belaney, 1888-1938
BAIRD — The story of John Logie Baird, 1888-1946
HUMGRUFFIN — A story of country folk . . . and giants
THE LOVERS' SEAT — The history and the love story of 1786. Fact and fiction
KIPLING — Rudyard Kipling, 1865-1936. An introduction
AN INTRODUCTION TO HASTINGS & ST LEONARDS
AN INTRODUCTION TO BEXHILL-ON-SEA
AN INTRODUCTION TO BATTLE, RYE AND THE VILLAGES

Preface

Of all the wonderful history of the county of Sussex, none has intrigued me more, nor given more pleasure, than the exploits of the colourful 19th century squire, John (Jack) Fuller of Brightling.

The seeds of interest were sown over 30 years ago while serving my apprenticeship in the printing industry in Hastings, when a working colleague and resident of Brightling would tell me wonderful tales from his village. How I relished those stories of a mad squire who built strange buildings with underground tunnels and the fanciful tales of smuggling and illicit gambling sessions in mysterious garden temples!

They prompted me to make my first visit to Brightling and, although I soon discovered that many of the stories were wildly exaggerated, I have never stopped returning to what I consider to be one of the most delightful and fascinating places in the country.

In 1979, my daughter was asked to write, as part of an English project at school, a short history of a local worthy. At my suggestion she chose John Fuller of Brightling. I found while helping her I became even more engrossed.

In the course of my research I contacted Mrs Rosemary Grissell, the then owner of Brightling Park (Fuller's home). She was able to give me valuable assistance and largely due to her encouragement and help, I produced a small booklet in 1983.

However, it did not end there! I later felt the subject deserved a more comprehensive study; that more meat should be put on the bones of the earlier publication with a greater use of illustrations to support the text. This book is the result.

Although John Fuller is best remembered in Sussex for the whimsical odd-shaped folly buildings which litter the village of Brightling, there were far more significant achievements.

Over the past years I have made many new friends through my interest in John Fuller and the subject has continued to prove both absorbing and rewarding. I hope you, the reader, will find it just as fascinating.

Come with me on a journey to the colourful, eccentric days of Georgian England. Come with me to the days of one of the great characters of Sussex past.

Come with me to the world of Squire John Fuller.

Geoff Hutchinson, 1993

THE TIME

John Fuller was a wealthy country squire, a Member of Parliament and owner of Sussex estates, London properties and Jamaican plantations. He was born into an influential family in 1757 during the reign of George II and died in 1834 at the age of 77. During his later years he became a much-respected philanthropist.

It would appear that John Fuller possessed an almost obsessive desire to be remembered by future generations. Throughout his long and eventful life he strove in various ways — some frivolous, some profound — to make a memorable contribution. He has succeeded.

He was a man very much guided by the eccentricities of his times and Georgian England provided the perfect platform for his larger-than-life personality. It was one of the most colourful, progressive and splendidly eccentric periods of British history. John Fuller played his part to the full and it is fitting to start his story with a brief look at some aspects of the society in which he lived.

The Georgian era had begun in 1714 with the accession of the first of the Hanoverian kings, George I and lasted over a hundred years until the death of King George IV in 1830. At the beginning of the period, Britain was already an important manufacturing country, most of the work being done by hand, but in the latter half of the 18th century, it became the most efficient trading force in the world with the introduction of machinery. This machinery was at first driven by water power and later by steam and this transformation of Britain's manufacturing methods became known as the Industrial Revolution. To fuel this great industrial expansion, the production of iron and coal increased dramatically.

One of the most important inventions of the times was the steam engine. Its greater power and reliability quickly put the previously-used water wheel into the shade. The first steam engine was built in 1769 by

James Watt and by the early 19th century steam-driven ships were in operation. Railway locomotives were soon to follow.

Most of the country was owned by a minority of rich landowners, who also controlled Parliamentary affairs and even in the early 19th century the landed gentry and aristocracy were still the most powerful political force, manipulating a grossly corrupt and unfair electoral system to protect their interests.

Many city merchants amassed great commercial fortunes and bought their way into the landed class and some exploited the mineral resources of their land to gain further wealth.

One of the most interesting features of the period was the dramatic growth in population. In 1700 there were an estimated six million people living in England and Wales. By the time of the first census in 1801 that figure had reached nine million and by the mid-19th century the population was over 18 million.

To feed this increase, farmers had to become more efficient. The countryside was transformed as the effects of what is known as the 'agrarian revolution' took shape. British farmers increased their output of crops and animal products, while employing fewer workers.

The ancient open-field system was substituted by more organised enclosed farming areas and inventions such as Jethro Tull's seed-drill enabled crops to be grown in greater density. Important advances were also made in stock breeding. The interest in improved farming methods was paramount in these times. Even King George III ran two farms at Windsor and Richmond and his interest in agricultural matters earned him the nickname 'Farmer George', a label he wore with much pride.

In 1801 over 70 per cent of the population lived in rural areas, where most gained their living from farming. But with the agricultural reorganisation and large-scale enclosure of land, the numbers of smallholders began to shrink with more people moving to urban areas to work. Large towns, especially in the north of the country, sprang up as the Industrial Revolution gained momentum.

Due to the poor state of the roads, goods were mainly transported by a network of canals, established to link the manufacturing centres. The only means of road transport was by horse and carriage and although the road system did improve slowly through the period, the fastest stagecoach journey between London and York took about four days.

For a third of the Georgian period, Britain was at war and as a result of continued successes the British Empire was beginning to expand. The British Navy was at the height of its prowess and played a vital role in the defence of the British Isles and the accrued colonies.

The Time

The Georgian period became renowned for the elegance of its grand houses and the laying-out of spectacular gardens. There was a surge of cultural interest among the more affluent of society and much colourful experimentation with architectural styles, derived from continental Europe — and beyond. Places such as Bath, Cheltenham and Buxton became great social and entertainment centres where the wealthy flocked to test the curative and relaxative qualities of the spa waters — and to enjoy themselves. Some of the best surviving Georgian architecture can be seen in these towns.

It was, however, an age of contrasts; the rich were very rich, the poor were very poor. There seemed no such thing as a middle class! Illiteracy among the poor was widespread and in the middle of the 18th century the average life-expectancy was just 37 years. The diet of the poor was very simple. The staple food was rye bread, cheese and butter and inexpensive meat was turned into broth. Fresh vegetables were consumed and tea and sugar were first introduced into the country. Ale and cheap gin were the main drinks of the poor. The rich often overindulged themselves on rich food. They ate vast quantities of beef, mutton, fish and game and drank the finest wines. Many gentlemen of the period suffered the agonies of the rheumatic disease, gout.

Britain's first iron bridge in Shropshire, opened in 1781. Today it serves as a striking reminder of the Industrial Revolution

The capital city reflected the shift to urban living. In 1750 London had a population of 675,000 but by 1851 it had risen to 2.3 million. By the end of the 18th century, although places such as Hammersmith were still just small villages and Shepherds Bush was grazing pasture, much of central London had developed to a pattern which is still recognisable today. Foreigners would remark favourably of the splendid shops and window displays in Oxford Street; Messrs Fortnum and Mason had joined forces in a grocery partnership; Mr Debenham was establishing himself as a draper; Hatchards were selling books; Chippendale and Hepplewhite were filling homes with elegant furniture; and Swan and Edgar opened their Regent Street store.

By 1802 Madame Tussaud, who had escaped from the French Revolution of 1789, had opened her waxworks in Baker Street and Thomas Lord had moved his Marylebone Cricket Club, founded in 1787, to St John's Wood and the site known ever since as Lord's.

Two great newspapers were established to cover events. *The Times* (The Thunderer) and *The Observer* were both founded towards the end of the 18th century.

Theatre-going was a popular pastime and regarded as one of the main delights of London life. Continental music was also popular in Georgian times and London provided a profitable stop-off for foreign musicians; the poets Byron, Shelley and Keats were coming to prominence; artists Turner and Constable were emerging and fashion trends were set by Beau Brummell.

At the beginning of the period, gentlemen wore three cornered hats over powdered wigs. Their coats were long with high collars that were usually worn open to reveal a brightly coloured waistcoat. On their legs they wore knee length breeches and on their feet, buckled shoes. Ladies wore full skirts and petticoats stretched over bustles. The fan was a popular accessory and hairstyles were elaborate and extravagant. By the end of the period styles had changed. Women's dresses became simpler in design with high waistlines while the gentlemen's attire was more like a riding outfit with top hat, tail-coat and tight trousers which were tucked into knee-length boots.

But it was not all elegance. As the gap between rich and poor widened, increased poverty forced many citizens to turn to crime. It was said of London by Horace Walpole: 'one is forced to travel even at noon as if one were going into battle'. The problem increased the number of offences punishable by death. By 1815 there were over 200 capital offences, which included minor theft of only a few shillings.

Smuggling was rife in Georgian times. Luxuries such as brandy,

A feature of Georgian England was its stunning architecture. Surviving examples can be found in many towns

tobacco and silk were often smuggled to avoid paying the high taxes. If caught, offenders were either hanged or transported. Tyburn Gallows (now Marble Arch), in London, was the scene of many public hangings.

The seeds of a properly organised police force had been sown in 1740 with the formation of the Bow Street Runners and in 1801 the river police were formed to combat dockside crime, but it would not be until 1829 that a regular police force was introduced.

Great advances were made in the sciences and medicine during Georgian times. Improvement in medical care was considered one of the contributory factors to the increase in population. Doctors were beginning to understand the workings of the human body and to learn more about the treatment of disease. Smallpox was the greatest killer disease of the 18th century but by 1808, thanks to the work of an English country doctor, Edward Jenner, it was being brought under control by vaccination. Over 150 new hospitals were built. Establishments such as Guys Hospital in London were used to train doctors and the need for bodies for research led to the appalling crime of bodysnatching from graveyards. Surgery was a very risky business. As there were no anaesthetics, surgeons had to work fast and many patients died of shock or through infection because of the lack of antiseptics.

There were other aspects of Georgian society which seem most abhorrent when viewed from this day. Slavery was still legitimate in the

West Indian colonies and its total abolition from the British Empire did not become final until 1833.

The most influential Christian body in the late 18th and early 19th centuries was the Church of England, but its attitude towards the poor was criticised by one of its own ministers, the Reverend John Wesley. He considered many of his colleagues were self-seeking and easily diverted from their duty to the community; more fond of leisure pursuits such as fox-hunting than saving souls.

It was against this background that John Wesley decided to take religion to the people. He rode thousands of miles around the country preaching in the open air to the poorer classes and by the time of his death, his Methodist religion had taken firm root.

Other Nonconformist groups such as Presbyterians, Baptists, Congregationalists and Quakers, although not as influential as the Methodists, were allowed to practise their beliefs. But for Roman Catholics it was a very different story. Until 1791 they were liable to persecution for merely practising their faith and they did not achieve political equality until the Catholic Relief Act of 1829. It was only then that Catholics were allowed to sit in Parliament and hold office under the Crown.

Many epic events took place during the period; the colonisation of Canada and India; the voyages of Captain Cook to New Zealand and Australia; the War of Independence and the loss of the American colonies by George III; the French Revolution; the Battle of Trafalgar; the Napoleonic wars which culminated in the Battle of Waterloo — to name but a few.

By the end of the Georgian age Britain had become an industrial giant and during the reign of William IV and later Queen Victoria, it was to grow even stronger with a succession of achievements. The British Empire grew still further under Victoria and the country approached probably the greatest period in its history.

It was against the lively, ever-changing backdrop of Georgian England that John Fuller would strive to perpetuate his name. His contribution was considerable and he was to become involved in many of the important issues of the day.

Although much of his time was spent in London, Fuller was never happier than when residing at his country estate, where he enjoyed his role as squire, presiding over the affairs of the local community. From the age of 20 until his death — and beyond — his name would be linked to a tiny village in the East Sussex countryside. It was a place very dear to his heart; a place on which he would leave his indelible mark.

THE PLACE

The East Sussex village of Brightling is five miles north-east of the market town of Battle, scene of the famous Battle of Hastings in 1066. It is situated high on a slope of a short range of hills with two tributaries of the River Rother, the Glothenham and Darwell streams, forming its eastern boundary. Many parts rise to a considerable height and there is said to be more woodland than in any other parish of the same size in England.

Brightling is a beautiful place, tranquil and unspoilt by the passing of time; a place where the visitor is rewarded with spectacular views across picturesque Sussex countryside; a place which holds a special kind of peace.

At the time of the Norman Conquest the area was devastated by the marauding army of William the Conqueror. In the later Domesday survey of 1086 the following entry can be found: 'The Count of Eu holds Brislinga. In the time of Edward the Confessor two brothers held it of the King. It was assessed for one hide then as now. On the demesne is one plough, and there is a church and woodland yielding five shillings.' The church mentioned was of Saxon origin and was probably of timber construction.

After William's conquest, the countryside was much changed as the land was divided into six rapes, each rape including a town, castle, river and forest. The Rape of Hastings was awarded to The Earl of Eu and he set about building a stone church at Brightling, dedicated to St Nicholas, to replace the timber structure. In Hastings Castle he erected a chapel and established a College of Prebendaries dividing the district into ten areas, one of which was Brightling.

The Archbishops of Canterbury were Deans of the College and Brightling Church was later re-dedicated to Thomas a Becket after his murder in 1170.

13

The advowson (the right of presentation to a church living) of Brightling remained in the hands of the Counts of Eu until the forfeiture of their estates in the reign of Henry III. At the time of the Dissolution of the Monasteries in 1539, it was given to Henry VIII's Master of Horse, Sir Anthony Browne, in whose family the patronage remained until 1633. Browne was also granted Battle Abbey as a gift from the king.

The area later became associated with the Sussex iron industry and today gypsum is mined, its operation carefully and tastefully hidden from view.

The village is dominated by the vast Brightling Park estate. Around 1695 it belonged to Edward English and in 1698 was sold to one Thomas Fuller, so beginning the association with Brightling of the great Sussex family, which was to put the village on the map. By the early 19th century the area would be turned into a magnet for those with an eye for the curious and unusual.

For added to its undoubted charm, Brightling has an air of mystery, which has caught the imagination of many thousands of visitors over the years. When travelling westwards on the main road through this quiet little place, approaching a sharp right hand bend in the road, there stands the parish church of St Thomas a Becket.

The Street, Brightling at the turn of the century

Nothing out of the ordinary about this, it seems. There are many pretty villages in the country with lovely old churches and picturesque churchyards. However, there is something very unusual about the churchyard at Brightling. For standing in the corner is a 25ft high pyramid, which from first impressions, appears to dwarf the church.

What is a pyramid of this size doing in a country churchyard? The onlooker cannot dismiss it as just an odd-shaped monument. It demands attention. One has to stop and look... and ponder over the reason for it being there.

Moving on through the village the traveller is confronted with other strange-shaped buildings dotted around the surrounding fields; a temple, an obelisk, a sugar loaf, a tower and even an observatory. What are they there for? Who was responsible for building them?

These architectural oddities of a bygone age are one of the best preserved groups of folly buildings in Britain. The pyramid in the churchyard is the last resting place of their creator, the village's most celebrated son, Squire John Fuller.

Many strange tales surround the pyramid, the best known of them states that he is sitting at a table inside, dressed in top hat, a chicken meal before him and that before he 'took residence' the floor of the tomb was scattered with glass to prevent the devil from entering.

15

A lovely story and one which has entertained many visitors through the years and although completely untrue, is typical of the tales surrounding the Squire of Brightling. The pyramid is John Fuller's last great statement — a monument to the eccentricity of his times. Ironically, it now marks the beginning of many people's fascination with this remarkable character of Sussex past. For after dismissing the myths and strange stories, one is still left with an undeniably mysterious fact about the structure, which makes one eager to learn more about its occupant.

The pyramid tomb was erected 24 years before his death!

THE SQUIRE

The two greatest influences on village life during the early part of the 19th century were the squire and the church. While the church administered to the spiritual needs of the community, the squire's great house in the park served as the administrational centre for village affairs.

The English squirearchy was firmly established during the 18th century when wealthy landlords, living in close contact with their tenants, took on the responsibility for the welfare of their communities. Among the squire's unpaid duties were the administering of justice, welfare of the poor within his parish and probably, most importantly, the initiation of improvements in farming methods on his estates. The great house would serve as estate office, temporary bank and courtroom, as well as providing elegant surroundings for grand social occasions.

The squire was considered to be the father-figure of the village — the person who drew the community together. A good squire would try to create a pleasant working relationship between himself and the tenant farmers who worked his land. This harmony relied on fairness and trust. The landowner would resist the temptation to charge exorbitant rents to his tenants, so enabling them to make a living and at the same time giving him a fair return on his investment. This created a balance which suited both sides. Most squires behaved in this responsible manner but, of course, there were exceptions. Some abused their authority and caused great misery, when unnecessarily raising rents, evicting tenants and repossessing land.

Fuller's grand house in the park, sketched by the famous landscape gardener, Humphry Repton, who prepared a report on the property in 1810

The most popular image of the village squire is described in books such as Henry Fielding's *Tom Jones*, where Squire Western is portrayed as a fair-minded man who loved fox-hunting, had a roguish eye for the ladies, was on nodding terms with all his villagers and was just as much at ease with his stableboys as with gentlemen of high breeding; a bulky, jolly, port drinking man, loud spoken and never afraid to forcibly express his opinions — but with a heart of gold.

It would appear John Fuller fitted this description and could be regarded as the epitome of the English country squire. He was a fair man. He followed the principle that if a landowner wished to improve the standard of agriculture he should reside more upon his estate and 'show more kindness and cordiality to the people instead of kicking and beating them about.'

Fuller was a popular figure in Brightling, much respected by the villagers and his tenants. To their delight — and sometimes confusion — he developed an eccentric strain, which is reflected in Brightling's best-known attractions, the odd structures he left scattered around the village for future generations to puzzle over. Due to these building extravagances, executed during the latter part of his life, he was fondly referred to as 'Mad Jack' Fuller. Some of his agricultural schemes were a little fanciful too and give us an insight to his inventive mind. In the East Sussex Records Office is a document giving instructions on how to grow grapes in cucumber frames and another shows a drawing of a device to 'prevent automatically water overflowing a pond.'

Eccentricity is a fascinating aspect of the human character and there is none better than the English for throwing up that peculiar tendency of breaking from convention. Strangely, it seems that many 19th century English squires were particularly prone to the condition; John Fuller was certainly not alone! Stories of their extravagant behaviour are legion, one of the most outrageous being the tale of Squire John Mytton who set fire to his nightgown to rid himself of hiccups.

However, it must be said that most of these so-called eccentrics (Fuller included), lived in a somewhat crazy age. For although Georgian England is best noted for its elegance, there were undoubtedly certain strange aspects in that society, which must have influenced people's thinking. For instance, at the very top, the monarch, King George III was considered (quite unfairly) to be mad, and the less-than-discreet, and sometimes downright outrageous, antics of his sons were causing public concern.

There was a peculiar quaintness about many things in Georgian England; everything seemed to be slightly off-centre and this trait appeared to spread right across the social scale. In what other age would you hear of an inquest being held in a public house into a man who died 'in a fit of laughing'? The verdict on Mr Blore, a master builder, who at least went to meet his maker with a smile on his face: 'Died by the visitation of God.' Or the gentleman who broke the law by burying his deceased wife in a shroud made of linen instead of the stipulated wool. He explained to the court that wool gave her a rash. He was promptly fined a shilling!

There were also many odd things happening in the field of building work and improvements. The country was in the midst of a great boom in experimental architecture and all types of influences were at force, based on the masters of continental and oriental design. The most stunning example which springs to mind is the Brighton Pavilion, completed around 1815 for the Prince Regent. Eccentricity was a way of life in Georgian England, especially among the landed gentry, who could afford to indulge in their whims and fancies. To be a trifle outrageous was acceptable and chic and it is best to think of John Fuller as a man guided by his times; a dedicated follower of fashion!

The squire's big house in the park reflected his leisured life-style and became the focal point for him to show off his wealth. Although many of these rich landowners were by no means intellectuals or astute judges of taste, they filled their houses with fine art collections, lavish furnishings and objets d'art collected from the European centres of culture. It was the thing to do! Most had extensive libraries and many experimented with the diverse fashionable architectural styles of the times.

The statement of wealth and power extended to the grounds surrounding their houses. The landscaping of gardens and parks and the building of eyecatching folly structures that decorated the estate and had no apparent purpose was commonplace. Again, it enabled the landowner to show off his taste — or lack of it — to outdo his neighbour and to leave a lasting monument.

With his wealth secured and after an eventful political career, Fuller saw fit to indulge in the popular pursuit of follybuilding. It was an expensive hobby and only the very wealthy could afford the luxury of adorning their grounds with oddities. It could be argued that during these times when much of the population was suffering extreme hardship, it was irresponsible to spend so much on buildings with such little practical use. However, in Fuller's case, it is said that most, if not all, of his follies were built to create employment.

For each folly there is at least one local story that has been handed down as to why it was built. Most are completely untrue. The local population of the time, not fully understanding the reason for a building being erected and having no access to it, would dream up their own story. As the years passed the stories have been distorted and sometimes the truth is very hard to establish.

John Fuller certainly had no problem financing his building projects. He was an immensely rich man.

So how did he gain the wealth to enable him to become a member of that exclusive fraternity of follybuilders? We need to look at the fascinating exploits of his ancestors to discover the answer.

BUILDERS OF FORTUNE

'Born with a silver spoon in his mouth': The term seems most appropriate when considering John Fuller's abundance of wealth. He was born into a family which, from relatively humble beginnings during the 16th century, had achieved great financial rewards in the county of Sussex and his immense fortune was the result of the endeavour of his ancestors. Throughout his long and eventful life he would be free to enjoy the fruits of their labours with no financial worries whatsoever.

The early history of the Fuller family is obscure, but the predecessors of the Brightling branch of the family tree can be traced to one John Fulwer or Fuller, a merchant citizen of London, whose descendant, also called John (a popular name with the Fullers), first resided in Sussex in 1575, when he acquired the unexpired lease of 'the manor and demesne of Tanners, Waldron', near Heathfield. The property was later bought outright.

There is no documented evidence of the trade followed by the first John Fuller of Tanners Manor, but it has been suggested that the family were involved in the cloth making trade and introduced water powered fulling (the cleaning and thickening of freshly woven cloth) to the county. Whatever their original occupation, the early Sussex Fullers were certainly determined to raise their social standing.

For much of England's history, the acquisition of land has been the most important source of wealth and this was undoubtedly the most efficient way to achieve status in the 16th and 17th centuries. The early Fullers were part of the growing number of city merchants who found the economic climate of the later Tudor years beneficial to their desire to branch into the country and use their profits to purchase land. They seized their opportunity with vigour. Their estates grew steadily over the years with the acquisition of land, farms and various properties across the county. Over 30 estates were added to the family's holdings during the first hundred years of their time in Sussex.

Waldron was to be the family base until the late 17th century. The village churchyard is the last resting place of many of the early Fullers, a fact noted with amusement by the Rev William John Humble-Crofts, rector of Waldron between 1882 and 1925, who wryly commented that the area could quite comfortably be renamed 'Fuller's Earth'.

An obvious means of generating further income from the acquired land was from farming and the family did this with great success. But it was from the middle of the 17th century that the first steps were taken which would lead to the Fullers becoming one of the most influential families in Sussex. In keeping with other ambitious landed families of the period they sought to exploit the mineral resources of their estates and from 1650 onwards turned their attention to the Sussex iron industry, which eventually resulted in the acquisition of land and the establishment of a large foundry close to Heathfield.

It seems strange these days to think that the beautiful East Sussex countryside of the Weald was once a vast industrial area, with giant furnaces setting the sky aglow; many villages and towns became cogs in the mighty iron industry. Iron founding had been carried out in Sussex as early as Roman times, but the 17th century saw a revival, which would last for a century and bring great wealth and prosperity to the area — and to the Fullers in particular.

At this time Britain's huge deposits of iron ore in the Midlands and north were practically unworked and the country's iron production was centred in the south and south-west. Sussex had ample quantities of iron ore and large forested areas which provided the charcoal necessary for the smelting and forging processes. Water was an important ingredient in the process and streams were dammed to create ponds which provided a power source for the blast furnaces and machinery.

Stimulated by the demands of war, merchandise from the Fuller foundry — mainly guns — was sold to the British Government and any surplus supplies were sold abroad. Surviving examples of cannons made at the Fuller Foundry and inscribed with the initials JF, can be seen at the Tower of London.

Casting was done in autumn, winter and spring and discontinued in summer months due to the low level of water. It was in summer that much of the merchandise was transported by wagon to the River Ouse at Lewes or the sea at Newhaven, or northwards to the River Medway, where it was shipped on the Tonbridge Navigation to Woolwich. Sussex

Tanners Manor — the Fuller family's first home in Sussex

roads were notoriously poor during the 17th century and the method of transportation by huge wagons, drawn by teams of packhorses, was clumsy, slow and dependent on good weather. If the summer was wet, the roads would quickly churn to mud and become impassable.

The problem of poor communications was not a new one. As early as 1584, Elizabeth I had passed an Act whereby ironmasters were ordered to pay a highway rate of three shillings for every ton of iron conveyed a distance of one mile along any road during the summer months. She also demanded the repair of any damaged roads as they went along their journey.

By the Fullers' time there were still levies to pay for use of roads and the less miles their wagons had to travel, the more profit they made. Judging by the total inaccuracy of the signposts which direct the modern visitor to Waldron it would appear the Fullers may have found a most convenient (and artful) way of overcoming the problem, by shrinking the mileage to an acceptable and economical level.

Due to the urgency of some of their orders the Fullers were prepared to risk transportation in the winter months. There were often accidents as wagons turned over, shedding their heavy loads. To try and alleviate the dangers it is believed a one-way system was operated in the Waldron area as the narrow lanes made the passing of two laden vehicles impossible. In the East Sussex Records Office are letters to clients in which the Fullers bemoan their plight. 'The ways are yet so bad that it is impossible to get anything to the sea side, those who have attempted it being laid fast,' wrote John Fuller in 1738. In 1743, after despatching 20 guns to Lewes, he remarked: 'They have torn the roads so that nothing can follow them and the county curses us heartily.'

However, these problems apart, the Fullers reaped good profits from the iron industry and with the continued success of their farming interests and increasing land ownership, they became the largest employer of the local community. In Heathfield half the population was employed in the Fuller foundry at the height of its trading.

The success of the Sussex iron industry reached its peak during the latter half of the 17th century and experienced a further revival around 1740 when extra demand for guns was prompted by the War of Austrian Succession (1743-1748). Profits from the gun-making operation for the year 1745/6 are shown as £2,365.2s.1d; the wages for men employed at the furnace ranged from £16 to £125 for a year's endeavour and they were only paid when the furnace was blowing.

In the late 17th century, the Fullers took residence at Brightling. Around 1698 Brightling Park was purchased by Thomas Fuller who, having no son of his own, conveyed it by deed of gift in 1705 to his nephew John, grandfather of 'Mad Jack' Fuller.

The Fuller coat of arms

John had two years previously married the heiress, Elizabeth Rose, the daughter of wealthy planter, Fulke Rose of Jamaica. Elizabeth's contribution to the marriage settlement was a large fortune and over 1500 acres of Jamaican plantations in the island's St Catherine's parish. A grateful John Fuller romantically renamed their Brightling residence Rose Hill in honour of his wife!

The marriage gave the Fuller family the added boost to lift itself still further up the social ladder. The importation of rum and sugar added another string to its bow — and yet more wealth into the coffers.

The Fullers had now reached country gentlemen status from their humble merchant origins and had acquired a coat of arms (usually the prerogative of nobility). It showed three bars and a canton with the crest of a lion's head mounted on a crown. The family motto was fitting: 'Carbone et Forcipibus'... By Charcoal and Tongs.

The marriage of John and Elizabeth produced 10 children. Three died while very young and six sons and one daughter survived. As well as raising this large family and administering the business affairs, John found time to become Member of Parliament for Sussex in 1713 in the last Parliament of Queen Anne and after failing to be re-elected in 1734, devoted much of his time to his local duties as squire and church warden at Brightling.

The offspring of John and Elizabeth were given every incentive for furtherance of their ambitions. The doors of opportunity were open wide and all profited from their parents' wealth to gain notable positions in society. The eldest son, yet another John, after attending Cambridge University, increasingly took over the running of the estates and, after his father's death in 1745, made considerable alterations and improvements to the house at Brightling.

The unusually-named second son, Rose, (one of the most interesting members of the family), qualified as a doctor after leaving Cambridge University and later went to Jamaica, where he was appointed as physician to the British troops on the island. He also managed the family's estates and became involved in the government of the island. On his return he became Member of Parliament for New Romney and then for Maidstone Borough and was a Fellow of the Royal Society. In 1768 he became Member for Rye and one of his major speeches in the House of Commons followed the Boston Tea Party incident in 1773, which preceded the American War of Independence. He was also instrumental in nurturing a strong West Indian lobby in Parliament and among his other interests was the running and welfare of the Foundling Hospital in Bloomsbury.

Stephen became a Fellow of Trinity College, Cambridge before taking up his post as London agent for the family's sugar importing interests, Thomas also entered the sugar trade and Hans was apprenticed to merchants in Lisbon, where he later died of smallpox. Henry (the father of the subject of this book) attended Cambridge University and later became a member of the clergy, while Elizabeth managed the household affairs after the death of her mother in 1728 until her marriage in 1733 to William Sloane. William was the son of Elizabeth, the widow of Fulke Rose, who had re-married a year after her husband's death, Dr Hans Sloane, founder of the Sloane Collection at the British

The first Fullers of Brightling. Standing, left to right: Rose, Elizabeth, Thomas, Hans, John junior, Henry (Jack Fuller's father), Stephen. Seated: John Fuller senior and his wife Elizabeth

Museum. The Fullers' association with the Sloane family, which they greatly treasured, was to last for many years.

Throughout the years of their involvement with iron, the Fullers still maintained their farming interests and were always keen to take advantage of the benefits of improved techniques.

However, the chief source of their income until near the end of the 18th century was iron. From this time onwards, for a variety of reasons, the Sussex industry began its decline. The southern forests were gradually becoming exhausted, the iron ore was having to be mined at lower levels and the cost of retrieving it was proving uneconomical.

Improved technology also played a part. Although coke, derived from coal, had been used to smelt iron from the beginning of the 18th century, it was not until around 1760 (the beginning of the most intense activity of the Industrial Revolution), that this became a perfected and common practice. Coke was used instead of charcoal and the huge supplies of coal in the Midlands and north meant that the industry moved to those areas.

Another factor in the decline of the Fuller Foundry was the inability to comply to the more precise specifications laid down for gun making. Larger guns were required and the resources of the Sussex workforce were unable to meet the production demands. There was also the increasing problem of transporting even heavier loads on inadequate highways.

The Fuller family's fruitful involvement in the Sussex iron industry ceased around 1765, when the decision was taken by Rose Fuller, who had by that date inherited the estates from his brother John, to run down the Heathfield operation.

It was time for the Fullers to take a detached but interested — and possibly amused — view of the iron industry as the great northern ironmasters emerged during the peak of the Industrial Revolution; eccentrics such as John 'Iron Mad' Wilkinson, who envisaged the coming of iron ships, railroads, iron houses and was fittingly buried in an iron coffin; John Roebuck, who founded the Carron ironworks in 1760, whose most famous products were the great guns known as Carronades, which were far superior to anything the Fullers could ever have hoped to have produced.

There were many more ironmasters to find fame and fortune in the heady days of the Industrial Revolution, but the Fullers' involvement in the industry, which had lasted for over a hundred years, had ended.

They had made their wealth at the opportune moment and perhaps, considering their previously mentioned problems, there may have even been a sense of relief to unload the burden.

However, a fortune had been amassed, invested and was to pass to future generations.

The Fullers of Brightling had become a force to be reckoned with; from humble beginnings, and after two centuries of earnest endeavour, skilful dealing and, of course, an element of good fortune in their marital arrangements, they had emerged from the lower commercial classes to form an important and influential squirearchy in the county of Sussex.

SON OF A PREACHER

For the purposes of this book it is necessary to take a closer look at the fortunes of Henry Fuller, the third son of John and Elizabeth Fuller of Rose Hill, Brightling and father of John (Jack) Fuller.

After attending Charterhouse School, London from 1726 till 1730, Henry went on to Cambridge University, where he graduated with an MA from Trinity College in 1739. On completion of his education he helped in the running of the family business and by 1743 was responsible for the collection of estate rents. However, his real ambition was to enter the Church and his father, using his wealth and influence, took considerable time and effort to help him secure a position.

By the mid-18th century, the tentacles of the Fuller family had spread to Hampshire; Henry's sister Elizabeth and her husband William Sloane had made their home at South Stoneham near Southampton and it was in this area, to the north of the city, that John Fuller concentrated his efforts on behalf of his son.

The advowsons of Broughton; St Mary's, Southampton; Mottisfont; Lockerly and North Stoneham all came under consideration, but all attempts to settle Henry proved problematic and the matter was not resolved before John Fuller's death in 1745. From his father's will Henry received £5000 as well as the right and title to the first vacancy in the livings of Mottisfont-cum-Lockerly and North Stoneham, with an additional £1000 if he did not take holy orders.

Henry was eventually presented to the Rectory of North Stoneham and Stoneham Abbots, near Southampton. King George II was named as patron in his induction mandate and he was installed as Rector on September 12, 1749 at the Parish Church of St Nicholas. He was to serve for the next 11 years.

The grave of Jack Fuller's parents, Henry and Frances Fuller. It is situated within St Nicholas Church, North Stoneham, Hampshire, where Henry Fuller served as rector for 11 years.

During this time he married his cousin, Frances, who was the daughter and wealthy heiress of Thomas Fuller of Park Gate, Catsfield. Between the years 1751 and 1753 they had two daughters, Elizabeth and Frances but, sadly for Henry, no son and heir. Evidence of Henry's desire for a son can be gleaned from his will, signed December 25, 1755. After its rather dramatic opening: 'I give my body to worms and my soul to the blessed Saviour of Souls', the will made provision for his wife and daughters and later implied Henry's desire for a son to follow in his clerical footsteps. He referred to the advowson of Mottisfont, which by this date had also come into his possession: 'If I should die without a son but should my dear wife at the time of my decease be with child of a son or sons, daughter or daughters, then my will is if it should be a son that the said living be kept in my family for his proper use and maintenance'. He went on to state that should his son 'take orders and over and above the said living I give and bequeath to my said son the sum of one thousand pounds for his maintenance till he shall come into the possession of the said living'.

In 1757 Henry's prayers for an heir were answered. John (Jack) Fuller was born on February 20. Sadly, he was to have little time to share with his son. The Reverend Henry Fuller died on July 23, 1761 at the age of 48, before young John had reached the age of five. It has been suggested that this loss at such a young age and the lack of a steadying influence and firm fatherly control could well have led to John's subsequent eccentricities. Another theory put forward is that the inter-marrying which took place in the Fuller family could have been a contributory cause. However, as previously discussed, it is probably much more feasible to accept that John Fuller's eventual so-called eccentricity was a product of his times and more allied to his great wealth.

Henry Fuller must have known his death was imminent in 1761. On July 16, just seven days before he died, he drew up a codicil to his will in which he made provisions for his children's education by stating that he wished a 'desk woman' (tutor) to be employed and that later young John be given 'a learned education and be brought up at Eton'. Henry also declared that John should have the sum of £1000, as soon as he reached the age of nine, to finance his time at the college.

So, after his initial education under the watchful eye of his female tutor, John, at the age of 10 years, was sent to Eton College, where he stayed till 1774. Eton, originally founded to train young men for the Church, later became renowned as a preparatory establishment for those intent on service to the State and although John did not follow his father into holy orders, Eton would almost certainly have benefited his later political aspirations. In the then spartan surroundings of the college, he would have met boys of a similar social standing, learned Latin and Greek and received a privileged education which would have set him fair for the future.

Unlike previous members of his family he did not go on to university and nothing is known of his whereabouts in the following three years. Due to this apparent elusiveness, his movements can only be surmised. As he was already quite a wealthy young man, perhaps he could see no purpose in striving for further education; he must have been reasonably confident that from somewhere in the great Fuller fortune, he would become even richer. Perhaps he followed the course of many of his contemporaries and filled the years by taking The Grand Tour of Europe, considered to be very much a part of a young Georgian gentleman's education.

In 1777 any hopes he may have had for increased wealth were well and truly realised. His fortune and future were secured when his uncle Rose died and having no direct heir, willed to him the Sussex estates and Jamaican interests. John Fuller took immediate possession of Rose Hill at the age of 20 and in all his varying roles and changing moods, would be associated with Brightling for the next 57 years.

His mother died a year after his inheritance, at North Stoneham, where she had remained since her husband's death. She is buried beside him in St Nicholas' Church. John, along with his two sisters, benefited greatly from her will.

At Rose Hill Fuller began to build his reputation as the approachable, fair-minded squire of Brightling. His higher education enabled him to master a working knowledge of the running of estates and to help administer the needs of villagers. For his leisure he enjoyed the normal country pursuits of wealthy landowners; foxhunting, shooting and hosting lavish parties in the great house.

As well as Rose Hill and his other country estates in Sussex, Fuller owned property in London and his great wealth also enabled him to enjoy a stylish urban lifestyle. In 1781 he owned a house in Wimpole Street and his sisters lived nearby in Welbeck Street. In 1798 he took possession of 36 Devonshire Place.

All these addresses were synonymous with the height of Georgian elegance and convenience; distinctive terraced houses, with every amenity. Each house had servants and separate accommodation at the rear — the mews — for coachmen, horses and carriages.

Throughout his life Fuller followed a family tradition with his love of music (his father and uncles had been schooled in the art of violin and spinet) and often held evenings of entertainment at his London homes. Many important artistes of the day performed for him, including the international tenor John Braham, who was a frequent guest. Braham was a composer of popular songs of the period, his most famous being 'The Death of Nelson', the proceeds from which enabled him to build St James' Theatre in King Street, London.

Fuller shared his time between his London and Brightling homes and enjoyed all the benefits his vast wealth could bring.

It was a grand life!

Fuller's London home in Devonshire Place

POLITICS: THE FIRST STEPS

In the year 1780, 22-year-old John Fuller, was to make his first excursion into the world of politics when, despite his tender age and the fact that he was little known in the area, he became Member of Parliament for Southampton Borough.

As we have seen, the Fuller family were no strangers to politics. Both John's grandfather and uncle had been Tory Members of Parliament during the 18th century and it seemed a natural progression for the wealthy young squire to take his place among the elite group which formed the House of Commons.

Fuller was delighted. In January 1780 he wrote enthusiastically from Southampton to his cousin John Trayton Fuller 'I flatter myself you will be happy to hear I have succeeded to the utmost of my wishes here.' Fuller had achieved his success largely due to the influence of his connections in the area. His cousin, Hans Sloane, himself a Member of Parliament, introduced Fuller to the voters of Southampton at a bye-election at the beginning of 1780. The election had been caused by the suicide of the serving Member, Hans Stanley, Sloane's uncle. It was very much a family affair!

In the 18th century Southampton was described as an open borough with a strong Tory interest and conditions had been most favourable for Fuller. Many of its former representatives had been country gentlemen of Hampshire or its adjacent counties and many, like Fuller, were owners of property in the West Indies. Fuller also became a freemason in Southampton, when he was initiated into the Concord Lodge. All these factors may have been instrumental in his election, but the most important requirement for a prospective candidate in Georgian times was wealth.

For in the late 18th and early 19th centuries the aristocracy and gentry still made up the most powerful political force in the country and a seat in Parliament was the almost exclusive right of the landed classes. To serve in Parliament was often regarded as an adjunct to social status as well as being the passport to a lucrative career and it also enabled the landowner to protect his interests.

Although there were no nationally organised political parties, the main factions in Fuller's day were the forerunners of today's Conservative and Liberal Parties — the Tories and Whigs — which had their origins in the religious feuds of the 17th century during the reign of Charles II. Both names were terms of abuse levelled against each other. The Whigs (derived from the word whiggamore - Scottish cattle drover), although led by the nobility, appealed to the interests of commerce and the professions, whereas the Tories (Irish bandits) consisted mainly of the landed gentry (especially the squirearchy), and the clergy and emerged as staunch supporters of the Crown and the Church of England.

The Whigs were the dominant force during most of the 18th century, until George III came to the throne in 1760, when the Tories gradually regained respectability. Around this time an added complication emerged when the name 'Tory' was applied by Whigs to other Whigs, whose views made them particularly acceptable to the king.

At this stage of Britain's history there was no voice for the middle or lower classes in Parliament. Only one in 20 of the population was entitled to vote and the unrepresentative electoral system was skilfully — and corruptly — manipulated by the landed gentry.

Many large towns, which were springing up during the Industrial Revolution, especially in the north, had no representative at all, whereas tiny places, once important but now practically uninhabited, still returned Members. A prime example was Old Sarum in Wiltshire, once a sizeable settlement, which had just seven voters. Another was Dunwich, which returned a Member, despite the fact it had long since disappeared under the sea. Small towns such as Winchelsea and Rye in East Sussex also returned two members. Fifty-six towns had less than 40 voters apiece. These were known as 'rotten boroughs'. Another equally corrupt means of gaining a seat in Parliament was through a 'pocket borough'. These constituencies were controlled by wealthy landowners and the handful of voters did as they were bid in exchange for favours.

Several abortive attempts were made to reform the electoral system during the late 18th century, when proposed Parliamentary Bills were strongly opposed and heavily defeated by the landowners and real progress towards electoral reform did not take place until 1832.

From the accession of the Hanoverian line with King George I in 1714, the effective royal power over Parliament had decreased throughout the 18th century. Parliament had taken advantage of George I's unfamiliarity with the British way of life (he spoke no English and made no attempt to do so) and during the reign of George II, had further increased its responsibilities.

However, in 1760, Parliament was to confront a more determined force in the shape of George III. The first of the Hanoverian kings to be born and raised in England, the young George pressed for more say in Parliament. He was determined not to become a puppet to the politicians and insisted on exercising the constitutional powers that still legally remained to him, and in particular the choosing of his own ministers. Many Parliamentarians of the day considered the king to be a meddler in governmental affairs. After the disastrous failure of the Earl of Bute, the first Prime Minister chosen by the king, a compromise situation was created whereby Parliament could force the king to dismiss any minister of whom it disapproved.

As there were no organised political parties in Georgian times, voters were simply choosing Members of Parliament, who sought election on local or personal matters rather than great issues of national policy. Hence the House of Commons consisted of a great diversity of smaller groups, factions, and interests, mostly revolving around a distinguished nobleman. No group was big enough to hold a majority in the Commons in its own right and its chances of office usually depended on either securing the king's favour or by forming a temporary alliance with another group.

Failing this, the group had to curry favour of the 200 or so Members in the House of Commons who mostly prided themselves on their independent viewpoint. This left the king to exercise his discretion when appointing both the leading minister and the other ministers too.

When Fuller was introduced as candidate for Southampton Borough in 1780, it was expected that his great wealth would deter any challengers, but he was eventually opposed by a local man, the Recorder of Southampton, Cranley Kerby, whom he defeated by a majority of 124. At the General Election which followed later in 1780 Fuller stood alongside his cousin, Hans Sloane, in opposition to John Fleming of Stoneham, 'a gentleman of considerable fortune and independent principles'. After a hard contest, in which the first two past the post were elected to Parliament, both Fuller and Sloane were returned by a small margin. The poll read: Fuller 264, Sloane 249 and Fleming 237.

And so Fuller took his place at the Houses of Parliament. Although in 1780 they were situated on the site we know so well today, the familiar sight of the Houses of Parliament with its commanding Big Ben clock tower, did not exist. The present buildings were not erected until 1834, after a fire destroyed much of the original Palace of Westminster.

In Fuller's time the House of Commons held their debates in St Stephen's Chapel which, with modifications, had been used for the purpose for nearly 300 years. The area now is known as St Stephen's Hall and serves as the main entrance hall, which leads to the present chamber.

Judging by some of the stories of Parliamentary life in the 18th and 19th centuries, it would appear the debating chamber of the House of

36

The 18th century debating chamber of the Commons. William Pitt, who became the country's youngest ever Prime Minister at the age of 24, addresses the packed House

Commons had an even more 'bear garden' atmosphere than today. Members would stretch out on the benches, cracking nuts, eating oranges, apples, pears and biscuits. What was spilt on the floor would provide food for the rats which took up occupation of the building after the day's business.

Whereas today's Mr Speaker would object most strongly to the introduction of alcohol into the chamber, in Georgian days 'a drop of the hard stuff' appeared to have a significant bearing on many of the proceedings. Even the young Prime Minister Pitt, early in his political career once had to leave the chamber during an important debate to be violently sick as the result of consuming too much port. In order not to miss anything that was said he vomited behind the Speaker's chair,

37

before tottering back to resume his part in the debate. Another story concerns Mr Speaker, who had a screen drawn across in front of his chair, behind which he would answer the call of nature.

But for all its faults, deficiencies and corruption, the House of Commons surprisingly worked very well and Fuller entered the political arena at a time when the country was passing through one of its most traumatic periods. The Prime Minister of the time was Lord North, who had enjoyed a long period of office but, unfortunately for him, had blundered — with the king's support — into the War of American Independence. Much of the fighting had gone badly and Britain's European enemies had begun to help the American rebels. In 1781 one of the main British armies had to surrender to the rebels at Yorktown; the colonies were lost and the United States of America came into being. As a result, North's ministry sank into decline, ending in his resignation in 1782.

There then followed a period of frequent change as one Ministry followed another over the following year, culminating in a coalition, (much despised by the king), between North and his former archenemy, Charles Fox.

Both Fuller and Sloane had supported North's administration until its end, but subsequently Fuller turned against the Fox-North coalition on one occasion and also absented himself from a division over the India Bill, which was introduced to establish greater control over the East India Company by the Government.

The fall of the Fox-North coalition was cleverly manipulated by George III and his next appointment of Prime Minister, in 1783, proved to be one of his most successful — William Pitt the Younger, who brought a period of much-needed stability and became one of the most influential political figures of the age.

Pitt's new Ministry seemed unable to classify Sloane's and Fuller's allegiance and ended up regarding them as opponents either to be won over or ousted. There is a popular story that at some time during his political career, Fuller was offered a peerage by William Pitt, presumably either to encourage his support or to get rid of him. Fuller is said to have declined the offer adding: 'I was born Jack Fuller and Jack Fuller I'll die.' Perhaps it was around this time the offer was made, although the two men were to meet up again in Parliament in later years.

At the General Election of 1784 neither Fuller nor Sloane put themselves forward for election and John Fuller's first brief excursion into politics was over. There would be a gap of 17 years before he would take up the political challenge again.

THE GENTLEMAN SOLDIER

Some ride in Yeomanry, some march on foot,
Some guides go forth, and some with rifles shoot.
Let Bony come with ship-loads of mounseers,
He'll stand no chance against such volunteers!

In 1798 John Fuller turned his attention to military matters when he became a captain in the Volunteer Sussex Yeomanry Cavalry, with 39 men under his command. The famous authoress and diarist of the times, Fanny Burney, implied in rather derisory manner, that Mr Fuller was devoting all of his time and attention to playing at soldiers. Perhaps she should have been less disparaging. To Fuller it was a serious business. He played an enthusiastic part in what he considered to be an invaluable contribution towards the defence of his country.

During the Napoleonic Wars against France between 1793 and 1815, there was a real threat of invasion and the counties closest to the coast felt, quite justifiably, that should such an invasion materialise, they would bear the full brunt of the attack. As a consequence the Government took defensive precautions with the building of fortifications; Martello towers were erected and elaborate signalling systems were set up along the coast.

But most significantly, the numbers of soldiers required to defend the coast were considerably increased and to complement the regular forces, local troops of volunteers were formed. These forces were a vital link in the defence of the coast because there was never enough regular soldiers to adequately cover the area. A modern-day comparison can be drawn to the Home Guard of the Second World War. The Georgian volunteer groups, consisted of infantry, cavalry and sea fencibles and were commanded by members of the gentry. Sussex was fortunate to have many members of the landed classes who were willing to take on the running of the troops; yet another example of their voluntary administrational contribution to local affairs. The financing of the volunteers was met by Government funding and subscriptions from the wealthier classes. By 1801 there were around 24,000 volunteer cavalry in Great Britain.

An 1803 cartoon depicting British resistance to Napoleon.

Many of the aristocrats of the county also became involved with the volunteer movement, including the third Earl of Egremont who, although not being a professional soldier himself, saw it as part of his public duty. As well as raising his own cavalry and infantry troops, he became overall commander of the Sussex Yeomanry Cavalry. In this post he acted as the purseholder responsible for equipping troops across the county.

Fuller was captain of his own troop, which served the Brightling and Heathfield area. It was formed in 1798 and continued until 1802. Several of Fuller's letters to Egremont have been preserved. In a correspondence dated November 30, 1799 and sent from his Devonshire Place address, Fuller acknowledged the receipt of £120 (£3 per man) to equip his troops and in 1801 he informed his Lordship that his troop was again up to its original establishment of 40 men, comprising one lieutenant, one trumpeter, three sergeants, three corporals and 32 privates.

In 1803, Fuller took a position of command in the much larger Hastings Rape Troop, which consisted of 583 men. He served until its disbandment in 1806.

Fuller was not the only member of his family to be involved in the volunteer movement. His cousin, John Trayton Fuller raised two troops during 1794, one at East Grinstead and another at Eastbourne.

The Yeomanry Cavalry was looked upon as the elite of the volunteer force and was seen by some of the lesser gentry as a way of mixing with the aristocracy. Each trooper had to provide his own horse and weapon and in many cases serve without pay. Many people at the time shared Fanny Burney's cynicism and scepticism by doubting the usefulness of these amateur soldiers and thought the whole exercise was just a harmless amusement for the country gentlemen.

Perhaps that was partly true. The importance attached to dressing up in uniform did in some cases tend to be over-enthusiastically pursued. Nothing gave the part-time soldiers more pleasure than strutting about, showing off their attire to admiring female friends and relations. The uniforms were purchased by the captains, who had the cost reimbursed from the county subscription fund. If they wished for a more elaborate uniform or more finery for their men, they were obliged to settle the difference from their own pockets. Many did and uniforms became more and more dressy and far less practical.

It would appear, however, that Captain Fuller did not subscribe to notions of fancy uniforms and once ridiculed the scantiness of dress of other regiments. He declared in typically forthright Fullerian fashion that the trousers worn by some soldiers were so tight that a sudden shower of rain would cause them to contract and split and 'the poor fellows were left with nothing but their shirts to cover a part of their bodies which, through modesty, I would not name'.

After their initial basic training, the volunteers would be put through regular drill sessions and mock battles to keep themselves honed for the real thing. These contrived skirmishes were usually conducted in a light-hearted fashion and were often just an excuse for a social gathering. They invariably ended in a draw with both sides sitting down together afterwards and overindulging themselves on food and drink. Hence, the early volunteer movement gained a reputation for a lack of organisation and discipline, but from 1803 onwards, increased efforts were made to improve efficiency.

By 1805 the threat from Napoleon had started to wane. His fleet had been defeated at the Battle of Trafalgar and his troops had been moved from the French coast to fight elsewhere in Europe. During the following year the majority of the volunteer troops were disbanded.

For all the organisation that went into the formation of these volunteer forces, they were never called into serious action. Apart from one solitary incident when a small French party landed in Wales and was swiftly dealt with by the local volunteer forces, Napoleon's threatened crossing of the English Channel and consequent invasion of this country never materialised.

However, Napoleon could gain some degree of satisfaction from the fact that England had been forced to spend huge sums of money preparing to resist him. Apart from the financing of extra troops, 74 Martello towers (nicknamed 'bulldogs' by the French), were built along the south eastern coastline. They were most numerous in the 16-mile stretch between Hastings and Eastbourne, where 31 were erected. They were positioned to provide total cover by gun-fire and the tapered shape was designed to deflect cannon shot. Each tower was topped by a large gun. They were a formidable and expensive means of defence.

But perhaps the most bizarre — and costly — defensive scheme dreamed up by the Government of the day was the Royal Military Canal, which stretches from Hythe in Kent to Pett Level in Sussex, a distance of 23 miles. It proved to be one of the greatest engineering follies ever. The intention of the 30ft wide canal was to resist the French advance. Sir John Rennie, the accomplished engineer, was put in charge of its building by Prime Minister Pitt and it was not until the project was near completion that its usefulness was analysed. It was then appreciated — too late — that any army which had crossed the great rivers of Europe, plus the English Channel, would hardly be deterred by a 30ft ditch. It had cost a staggering £200,000!

Apart from his part-time soldiering, there had been other things happening in John Fuller's life. His two sisters had both married into high society; Elizabeth to Sir John Palmer-Acland, and Frances to Sir Lancelot Brown, the son of the famous landscape gardener, Capability Brown.

But the wedding bells would never sound for John Fuller...

An officer of the Yeomanry Cavalry

ROMANCE AND REJECTION

The closest John Fuller came to marriage was when, at the age of 33, he proposed to a Miss Susanna Arabella Thrale. Susanna was in her early twenties at the time — and she declined his proposal. He was not amused!

The affair is mentioned in a letter written by Mrs Henrietta Henckell Hare, whilst touring Italy in 1790. Mrs Hare, who lived at nearby Herstmonceux Place was the wife of the Rev Robert Hare and an avid letter writer. Her gossipy correspondence to her sister in England has been preserved and provides the researcher with invaluable snippets of information from those times.

In the letter sent from Florence in October 1790, she stated: 'Mr and Mrs Brown (Miss Fuller that was) are at Pisa for the winter. I have not yet seen them.

'Our neighbour of Rose Hill has been lately I hear refused by Miss Susan Thrale. He is so angry with her that he has brought down a woman of the town to Tunbridge Wells on purpose to distress her by following her about everywhere. If this is the fact I think him a great fool.'

Just why Fuller was spurned by young Susanna is not recorded, but it did seem a rather peculiar way of exacting his revenge on her.

At the age of 33 Fuller would have been quite a catch for any young lady. He was rich, adequately educated, well versed in the etiquette of the times and was quite capable of mixing in the higher circles of society. Although a large man with an ever increasing waistline (a common problem among the Georgian elite), he was certainly not ugly.

Susanna was the sixth child of the Streatham brewing magnate, Henry Thrale and his wife Hester. The Thrales mixed in the highest echelons of society and became renowned and respected in the great social centres across the country. For many years they were associated with the famous diarist and political columnist, Dr Samuel Johnson, who accompanied the family on their many trips. Fanny Burney was also a close friend of the Thrales and a member of the 'Dr Johnson circle'.

Much information on the Thrale family can be gleaned from the comprehensive (and sometimes tragic) diary kept by Mrs Thrale, in which she documented the raising of her 12 children. Susanna was born in 1770, two months prematurely and her early life was fraught with illness. At birth, her mother described her as 'so very poor a creature I can scarcely bear to look on her', and the Reverend Evans said he had 'never christened so small a child before'. Dr Johnson was the only one to show admiration for her and assured all concerned that Susanna would grow to be a beautiful woman.

By the age of two there was certainly little improvement. Susanna was described as small, ugly and lean. Her frail body was racked with anaemia, rickets and a troublesome hernia and she was teasingly nicknamed 'little crab' by the other children of the family. At times there was grave concern for her survival. However, Dr Johnson's initial faith in her proved to be justified. As she grew older she shook off her ailments and developed into an attractive and confident woman.

It is quite possible Fuller first met her either in London or in the popular spa town of Tunbridge Wells, where the Thrale family would stop on their frequent journeys to their West Street property in Brighton.

Tunbridge Wells was one of the first spa towns and along with places such as Cheltenham, Buxton and Bath, became the haunt of wealthy city dwellers who, suffering from overindulgence in the capital, hoped to be cured by drinking the waters.

These towns also gained a reputation as meeting places for the sexes. Women, appreciating they could improve their social standing through marriage, used the local assembly rooms as marriage markets, where they would use their charms to attract wealthy suitors.

Susanna, however, was in a comfortable financial position in her own right, having inherited a sizeable sum of money after her father's death in 1781. By this date she had three surviving sisters, the eldest of whom, Hester, became Viscountess Keith.

Much to the displeasure of her daughters, Mrs Thrale eventually remarried in 1784. Although she had been reasonably happily married to Henry Thrale, she described her feelings towards her new partner, Italian singer Signor Piozzi, as 'the first time she had even been in love'.

Susanna Thrale

*Left: Dr Johnson.
Facing page: 18th
century Tunbridge
Wells, a social centre
and marriage market*

London society considered Piozzi a roguish adventurer; the cartoonists and columnists of the day pilloried her over her choice and declared he was only interested in her wealth. Her marriage was also greeted with disapproval by Johnson, who had made great efforts to dissuade her from taking what he considered to be an unwise step. But the critics' fears proved unfounded. Piozzi behaved impeccably and he and Mrs Thrale lived happily together for many years. However, her daughters never forgave her and the family was irrevocably split.

Why the relationship between Jack Fuller and Susanna Thrale failed to flourish can only be guessed at, but it would appear that Susanna was very hard to please. Apart from Fuller, Susanna attracted the attention of many other hopeful young gentlemen, including Lord Peterborough in 1794, but none won her hand. In 1795, she wrote to her sister in despairing fashion: 'there was not a tolerable man left in the county of Sussex'.

Susanna had even caught the eye of the Prince Regent but this time her interfering mother put a stop to events by refusing her permission to entertain him. Mrs Thrale said she could see 'no moral purpose being served' by allowing Susanna to receive the royal visitor. It was considered an act of great rudeness to His Royal Highness and further damaged Susanna's already strained relationship with her mother.

Fuller had been known to the Thrale family for several years. Indeed, in 1781 he had been a favourite of Susanna's elder sister, Hester. Mrs Thrale clearly disapproved. Writing in her diary on January 29 of that year, she stated in less than complimentary terms: 'Jack Fuller of all people! wild, gay, rich, loud, I wonder how a girl of delicacy can take a fancy to Jack Fuller of Rose-hill? no proposal however has been made, nor do they often meet; but I rather think she likes a boisterous character.' Later that year she wrote: 'Captain Fuller flashes away among us. How the boy loves rough merriment! the people all seem to keep out of his way for fear.' It would appear that Fuller was still in good shape around this time and had not yet put on weight. Fanny Burney was certainly impressed. She described him as 'having a good figure, understanding, education, vivacity and independence'.

Whatever the reasons for John Fuller's failure to capture the heart of Susanna Thrale, it proved in later years to be once bitten, twice shy. Although keeping a rakish eye for the ladies, he put all thoughts of marriage from his head and remained a bachelor for the rest of his life.

An interesting psychological theory was put forward by Mr Edward Shoosmith in a letter to the Sussex County Magazine of July 1933, in which he considers the reasons for Fuller never tying the matrimonial knot. He stated that Jack Fuller 'belonged to what modern psychoanalysts would term the virile archetype, displaying a permanent monogamous love which, to quote Gregorio Maranon's *The Evolution of Sex*, "represents the highest degree of perfection of human sexuality, since it represents the maximum of refinement of the libido and therefore the degree most remote from generic or cynical sexuality" elsewhere defined as "a fetishism of the ideal which raises it to a degree of ultra-perfection". Such men love only once, their swan-song at Cupid's bidding cast finally as a tragic sacrifice to the Bacchanalia of Venus'.

It appears a rather fanciful theory. Considering the morals of the upper classes of the time, it seems a trifle amusing to think of the full-bloodied, boisterous Fuller ever being interested in monogamous love or indeed, aspiring to a degree of ultra-perfection. Perhaps it is being a trifle unfair to him, but it seems most probable that the diary entries of many of the women he met (serving maids included), would have destroyed that particular theory.

Perhaps the 'woman of the town' he unleashed on poor Susanna Thrale to 'follow her about everywhere', could also have given a few more clues to his sexual preferences and provided a more accurate assessment of his libido!

And what became of Susanna Thrale? She never married, but in June 1807 she entered into a somewhat controversial arrangement when she took joint occupancy of Ashgrove Cottage, near Knockholt in Kent, with a 43-year-old watercolourist, William Frederick Wells. Wells was a close friend of the famous painter Turner and had lost his wife in the February of that year. Susanna helped to care for his seven children. Her family, not sure of the nature of the relationship with Wells, were far from happy with the situation.

Her association with Wells lasted only a few years and before 1820 she had taken over sole occupancy of Ashgrove Cottage, when Wells had moved away to Mitcham in Surrey.

She lived a quiet, reclusive life at Ashgrove Cottage until her death in 1858. During her time there she founded a school for the local children. Considering the unfortunate start to her life with her many life-threatening ailments, it seems remarkable that Susanna Arabella Thrale reached such advanced years. She died at the age of 88, a lonely but peaceful and contented spinster.

UNEXPLOITED WEALTH

John Fuller continued to administer his estates at Brightling in a responsible fashion and in 1796 was given one of the most prestigious offices available to country gentlemen — High Sheriff of Sussex, the king's legal representative for the county.

The term of office was one year and the post was considered a great privilege and held the unique distinction of personal (if short) association with the monarch. There was no salary and only the wealthiest could afford to take on the task. It was viewed as an ideal way of increasing a gentleman's social standing. Among the more pleasant of his duties would have been the attendance at courts across the county and the entertaining of many important and influential people from the legal profession.

However, it was not all fancy parties and privilege. There was a much more demanding side to the job as well. The sheriff, as Keeper of the King's Peace, bore part of the responsibility for trying to maintain law and order and in Fuller's day every section of society was plagued with a large criminal element.

The sheriff was responsible for raising the hue and cry and would have been empowered to raise a local militia if needs demanded. He was also required to attend executions. Fuller served his year's appointment with honour and style. His reputation was growing.

Fuller was always eager to increase the size of his holdings with the further acquisition of land, farms and properties. On the death of his uncle Rose, he had inherited a total of 5584 acres across Sussex, of which 1500 were at Rose Hill. During his time at Rose Hill he added a further 2033 acres to the Brightling estate and 59 acres elsewhere. His acquisitions spanned an area from Battle in the east to Burwash and Heathfield in the west. More land, more power!

The year 1801 was to be a most important one for Fuller but it also threw up a mystery. At one stage he was on the brink of returning part of his estates to the industrial past of his ironmaking forefathers. A seam of coal was discovered on his land between the parishes of Heathfield and Waldron. Initially there was much excitement and great expectations at the find, but the whole affair ended in confusion when the seam was not exploited.

Despite the fact that a local blacksmith had given his approval of the coal and said 'he had never worked more pleasantly or had a better fire', the reason given for non-exploitation of the seam was the high content of sulphur in the coal. Plans for production were shelved.

Years later, in 1830, more (but no less puzzling) light was thrown on the matter by a Mr Sylvan Harmer, in a letter to the *Brighton Guardian* newspaper in which he related the experiences of his late relative, Mr Jonathan Harmer who had in the month of December 1801 been employed to survey woods in the parishes of Heathfield and Waldron and had seen samples of black straten, which he considered to be coal of some description. The next day, 'with pick and shovel I laid open a block of jet-black and pure coal of the Kendal species'.

Jonathan Harmer informed Francis Newbury, then proprietor of Heathfield Park, of his find and was told to pack up the coals and send them to Mr Fuller in London. Fuller then sought the advice of Mr Ward, a Derbyshire miner, who suggested sinking a shaft, as he felt 'that all the signs and appearances were sufficient to inspire any miner with the greatest hopes'. But for some reason, Fuller surprisingly failed to act!

The financial advantages of owning land containing coal in the early 19th century, whatever the quality, were enormous. By this time coal was one of the vital factors responsible for generating the great mechanical age and pushing the country towards its peak of industrial power. Output in the country was rising dramatically as the Industrial Revolution gained pace. In 1800 the total was 11 million tonnes and by 1826 it had almost doubled. By 1880 it had reached a staggering 154 million tonnes.

Despite the fact that another Derbyshire miner had offered to stand half the cost of boring in the park, Fuller still refused to act. Perhaps he just could not be bothered. Perhaps he considered he was wealthy enough and did not wish to scar the land; perhaps there were legal problems. The continuing problem of transportation on poor roads could also have been a deciding factor. However, the most likely reason for his apparent lack of interest is that in 1801 he had other matters on his mind.

Earlier that year his attention had turned once more to Parliamentary affairs. After a break of 17 years he had resumed his role as politician and had taken his seat in the House of Commons.

TO SERVE FOR SUSSEX

In 1801 the Member of Parliament for Sussex County, Thomas Pelham, was called to the Upper House as Lord Pelham, so creating a vacancy in the House of Commons.

This meant the Sussex 'interests' had to search for a new Member to represent them and one man in particular had caught their eye. The scene was set for John Fuller, now aged 44 years, to make his return to the Parliamentary stage.

Little had changed in the corrupt electoral system, although the counties were considered to be the most representative, but even here the vote was only given to certain freeholders. Each county elected two Members to Parliament and they were usually nominated by powerful county families to stand in local elections. Usually no contest took place as the leading 'interests' in the county fixed it between themselves to have one Member each. These deals might have occurred between two great aristocrats or between an aristocrat and a body of the landed gentry or between Whigs and Tories.

In 1801, the electoral system was well suited to John Fuller's ambitions and his entry into Parliament was comparatively easy. He was invited to stand for 'election' by a distant relative, the influential Justice of the Peace, George Shiffner of Lewes, an ex-officer in the Dragoon Guards. Fuller's great wealth deterred any challengers and he took his seat in the House. A similar procedure was followed in the local elections of 1802 and 1806, when Fuller, again quite comfortably, retained his seat. His second term in Parliament must have given Fuller far more satisfaction than his first. He was now on home ground, representing his beloved Sussex.

Fuller re-entered the political arena at a time of great historic

The Duke of Wellington. John Fuller was one of his greatest admirers

importance. In 1801, the country was at a state of war with France and, but for a brief halt in hostilities in 1802, would remain that way through his political career and beyond. Napoleon Bonaparte was reaching the height of his prowess and posing a real threat of invasion. Great battles such as Trafalgar and Waterloo were fought and legendary heroes such as Nelson and Wellington were performing their acts of daring in the cause of their country. As previously mentioned, Fuller himself was playing his own part in the country's defence through his involvement in the Sussex Yeomanry Cavalry.

Henry Addington was the Prime Minister until 1804 when the irrepressible William Pitt the Younger served his second term until his death in 1806.

Being involved in Parliament must have strongly appealed to Fuller. Unlike some Members who just used their seat for personal gain and hardly ever attended the chamber, it would appear Fuller genuinely welcomed the opportunity of using the House to express his views. And express them he did — frequently!

By now he had certainly developed a more outspoken and outrageous streak to his character, which must have fitted in well in the sometimes chaotic surroundings of the House of Commons. His physical appearance was striking to say the least and he was certainly no follower of fashion when it came to dress. He had a liking for the rather dated powdered wigs and was one of the last men in the country to wear his hair in a pigtail. Through gross over-indulgence of rich food and drink (a common pursuit of wealthy squires of the time), his body was growing to massive proportions and although he had not reached his reputed maximum weight of 22 stones, he was nevertheless an extremely large domineering figure.

The intake of food by the upper and middle class Georgians provides some staggering statistics. Owing to increased production, food was so plentiful that they simply found it impossible to stop eating. It is said that one Yorkshire squire of the period consumed the following in just one sitting: A plate of haddock, another of veal, two of tongue, three of mutton, two of roast pig, a wing of duck, and half the tail of a lobster.

Dessert consisted of cheeses, oranges and nuts and the food was washed down with sherry, port, marsala and madeira, followed by a night-cap of brandy or gin with sugar. There is no reason to doubt that Fuller's diet followed a similar pattern.

It was small wonder that the gentlemen of the period had extended waistlines and sported rosy cheeks and mottled noses.

Complementing his size Fuller possessed a loud booming voice, which served him well. With his lively, boisterous style he soon gained a reputation as the court jester of the House of Commons. His approach was blunt and sometimes coarse, yet he was still able to punctuate his oratory with quotations from Shakespeare. His speeches were short and to the point. There were no pretentious labouring statements from Mr Fuller. His attitude is perfectly summed up in the following: 'When I do get up, I speak to the subject, aye, and pretty freely too. As to the people who make fine speeches and clap their hands upon their hearts, they might as well clap them anywhere else.'

Lord Nelson, another great favourite of John Fuller. It is believed the two men became acquainted during Fuller's time as a Jamaican plantation owner

Everything he did seemed to have an air of flamboyance. Journeys from Brightling to his London home during Parliamentary sessions were nothing short of pantomime. He would ride in the stylish family barouche, drawn by four large horses. The Fuller coat of arms was proudly displayed on the doors of the coach, which was usually packed with provisions and protected by armed coachmen and footmen carrying pistols and swords. It must have made a stirring sight when Jack Fuller arrived in town!

It would appear he was a popular figure at the House of Commons who was much respected for his honesty. He became known as 'Honest John', a title which gave him much pleasure. Although taking his seat under the Tory banner, he prided himself on his independent viewpoint. He once told the House that he was never an admirer of affected piety and he never decided upon any question without informing himself upon it, as well as he could and he 'always found it the safest way to be guided by the sentiments without doors, rather than the professions made within.' With his ego somewhat inflated, he then suggested to both sides of the House that 'they should consult with honest, impartial men like himself to enable them to form a just and fair decision.'

Some Members found Fuller's self-professed honesty a little hard to bear. They thought him too fond of blowing his own trumpet. One Member was known to remark with measured sarcasm that Fuller thought he monopolised the whole political honesty of the House. Fuller's reply was typically brusque!

Throughout his political career and beyond Fuller maintained a passionate loyalty to the Crown and was a staunch supporter of the principles of the Church of England. Overall, his spell in Parliament between 1801 and 1807 was a happy one. He was considered a well-behaved Member who, although possessing a forceful and excitable nature, attracted little controversy.

That was to come later . . .

A Bitter Contest

At the General Election of 1807, John Fuller found his previously easy passage to Parliament had deserted him and he was involved in a tough struggle to retain his seat. No gentleman's agreement this time; just stiff competition.

For occasionally there could be a slip up in the type of gentleman's agreements which had secured his seat in earlier years. This occurred when a Whig actually opposed a Tory and their differing views and strength of commitment to a particular cause, prevented any hope of a compromise or deal being struck between them. Such was the case in Sussex in 1807.

Such an occurrence could prove costly and the 1807 General Election threw up more than one of these expensive confrontations. Both Fuller and his opponent were obliged to lay out substantial sums of money as their bitter campaign gained momentum.

In Sussex there were two seats to be contested; one for the west of the county and the other for the east. Under the comfortable terms of the 'arrangement' system, the Hon Charles W Wyndham, a Tory and former captain of the Petworth Troop of the Sussex Yeomanry Cavalry, was the only candidate nominated for West Sussex and he was duly elected with 4,333 votes.

Fuller's opponent for the East Sussex seat was the Whig, Colonel Warden Sergison of Cuckfield, who proved to be a formidable adversary. The campaign was fought on two highly contentious and extremely sensitive issues of the day.

Sergison attacked Fuller over his refusal to vote against the abolition of slavery and Fuller countered with an anti-Popery attack against Sergison's support for the emancipation of Roman Catholics.

Fuller's support for slavery was aligned to his involvement in the Jamaican estates. He gained much benefit from it! The subject had occupied much of his thinking during the early Parliamentary years and many times he had leapt to its defence.

The use of slaves, shipped in appalling conditions from Africa to the West Indies to work in the sugar plantations, was commonplace and the sordid, degrading trade had prospered for many years. Much of Britain's 18th century trade, along with the Dutch, French and Portuguese, who were responsible for instigating the first slave market in Europe at the port of Lagos, depended heavily on slave labour and the British economy thrived on what was referred to as the 'triangular trade'. Cotton goods were shipped from Liverpool, London or Bristol to Africa, where slaves would be loaded for the journey to the West Indies. The ships would then return to Britain with raw cotton, sugar and tobacco, ready to start the cycle again.

The sea journey for the slaves was almost unimaginable. Chained together on the lower decks, with no privacy and little or no headroom, they would spend most of the six week voyage in a crouched position. Periodically they were taken to the upper deck for exercise, which normally consisted of lashing them until they jumped up and down in their chains.

The scale of the horrendous trade was enormous. Britain alone transported 50,000 slaves during the year of 1771. On reaching the West Indies, they were sold for up to £40 each and put to work in the plantations.

The plight of the slaves on these inhumane voyages was brought to the attention of Parliament in the late 18th century by the reformer William Wilberforce, who had devoted his life to the abolition of slavery. However, on his attempts to stem the trade, Prime Minister Pitt the Younger encountered fierce opposition from the powerful West Indian sugar interests who also expressed the fear that British shipping would suffer if its share of the trade were taken over by the French. After several abortive attempts to force through reform, the initially sympathetic Pitt abandoned his principles on the slave trade and it continued until 1807 when a law was passed prohibiting any British participation in the shipment of slaves and this was followed in 1815 with the abandonment by the European nations.

However, it was still legal to own slaves and the trade persisted with conditions in the slave-ships becoming even more appalling. Shipping lines, prepared to supply the demand and take the risk of breaking the law for vast profit, crammed yet more negroes into their ships. If they feared detection from an oncoming patrol ship, the slaves would be thrown overboard — chains and all.

Wilberforce, convinced that while slavery existed, there would always be slave trading, made determined efforts to intensify his anti-slavery campaign in 1832 and the following year Parliament voted to abolish slavery from the British Empire. All slaves were to be freed within twelve months and this shameful part of British commercial history would be gone forever.

Fuller had spoken out many times against the abolition of slavery during his time in the House. On May 30 1804, he stated that he considered the situation of the negroes in the West Indian colonies 'was equal, nay, superior to the condition of the labouring poor of this country. They were better fed and more comfortably accommodated'. He said he had letters in his pocket which assured him of the fact and he knew it from his own experience. He also maintained that their labour was not nearly so severe. 'The best of the negroes do not in general perform half as much labour as even the most indifferent of our labourers,' he said.

'It was not,' he argued, 'true that the negroes felt themselves miserable under English masters. The very reverse was the case, for they felt themselves happy under an English master and an English government.' He declared that he had given permission to his slaves to cultivate considerable spots of ground for themselves and ample time for the purpose. 'I have lodged and clothed them and have engaged a physician to attend and prescribe to them. I have done everything for their comfort.' He related that one of his slaves who had been with him for 20 years had lately given him £200 for his freedom.

The first European slave market at Lagos in Portugal

He admitted that the slave trade was not moral in nature or design, but thought it arose out of the peculiar circumstances in Africa. He commented on the 'tyranny of the native princes of Africa', and ridiculed the African mentality towards witchcraft. 'When the negroes got to the West Indies, they were sometimes not divested of these foolish notions. On my own estate I have been obliged to hang a negro for having killed four others on an imputation of witchcraft.'

In the months immediately preceding the General Election of 1807, the subject of reform was in its early stages and Fuller fought hard to resist the impending winds of change with added fervour. Many times he leapt to the defence of slavery. On March 6 1807 his voice boomed around the chamber: 'We might as well say, Oh we will not have our chimney swept, because it is a little troublesome to the boy, as that we should give up the benefit of the West Indies on account of the supposed hardships of the negro.' At every opportunity he tried to force his opinion upon the House, until in the April of that year he eventually fell foul of the Speaker when he raised the slavery issue during a debate on other matters. The Speaker swiftly put him in his place!

So vociferous were Fuller's protests that even several of his former supporters, seeing that his views were becoming increasingly isolated, became embarrassed by his attitude and found themselves unable to lend their support to him. At one stage in the lead up to the election, it was decided by the East Sussex 'interests' to invite another candidate to stand in Fuller's place and George Shiffner was the name suggested. Shiffner was placed in an awkward position. As already explained, he was distantly related to Fuller and had previously nominated him for Parliament in 1801.

Shiffner declined the invitation to stand and Fuller was left to put his unpopular ideas on slavery to the test.

Fuller became increasingly annoyed at efforts to discredit him with suggestions that he was using public funds to help maintain his Jamaican interests. He vigorously denied such accusations and forcibly stated that his family 'had never been indebted to any faction or to any Ministry for sixpence of the public money.'

Sergison made the slavery issue his main attack. He issued cleverly produced hard-hitting posters and leaflets in which he warned the Freeholders of Sussex to beware: 'He that is the advocate of Slavery in another country, would, probably, be glad to introduce the cruel and bloody system to his own — might rejoice at beholding even Britons in Chains!'

Another poster portrayed Fuller as the actor 'Rosy West Indian Jack',

ON MONDAY NEXT,
BY DESIRE OF THE AFRICAN TRADERS,
WILL BE ATTEMPTED AT
The Hustings Theatre, Lewes,
THE *CONDEMNED* TRAGEDY, CALLED,
SLAVERY !
The principal Character by the noted
Rosy West Indian Jack.
TO WHICH WILL BE ADDED

A new Melo drama, never performed here, called
Britannia in Tears !
Should the above pieces, however, be rejected, as offensive to the taste of free Born British Subjects, that the audience may not be disappointed,
Sprigs of Laurel,
IS IN REHERSAL,

In which an esteemed British Officer will make his appearance, whose every wish is to please, and deserve the patronage and support of his Countrymen.

Attree & Phillips, Printers, Herald Office, Brighton.

hard-hitting poster published by Sergison, attacking Fuller's support of slavery

AN ADDRESS TO THE PUBLIC.

You may say what you please
But FULLER hath done a very great Thing
In supporting the Crown, Constitution, and King.
When the Catholic Bill appeared in the dark,
He boldly opposed it with Loyalty's Heart.
Again he steps on as a Candidate true,
For Rights of his Country he still is true blue.
Tho' Snakes in the grass may hiss him about,
Yet with true manly Courage he'll see the Poll out.
For the Catholic Bill was a serious thing
Which aim'd at our Rights, Religion and King
Then come ye Freeholders your votes don't withhold
Be firm, never mind them, for Fuller be bold.
While George fills the throne may no Catholic sever.
Our good Constitution! Then FULLER for Ever!

But No Popery!

May 22, 1807.

BAXTER, PRINTER, LEWES.

Election poster published by Fuller

appearing in a 'condemned tragedy called Slavery'. Sergison cast himself as 'an esteemed British Officer' whose alternative production 'Sprigs of Laurel' (a reference to his anticipated election victory) would appeal better to the people of Sussex.

However, Sergison himself was also flying in the face of controversy with his campaign message. He was a supporter of the emancipation of Roman Catholics, who at this time had little say in the running of the country. It was an issue which deeply reflected the prejudices which dated back to Elizabethan times. In 1780 London had experienced severe civil unrest when the Protestant fanatic Lord George Gordon had led a mob to Parliament to demand the repeal of the Relief Act which allowed Catholics the right to purchase and inherit land. MPs postponed consideration of the mob's petition and angry Protestants vented their anger on Catholic property in the city. Looting and burning lasted for a week, with more than 400 deaths.

At the end of what became known as the Gordon Riots, 25 offenders were hanged and Gordon himself ended his days in an asylum.

The subject of Catholic emancipation rumbled on into the early 19th century. In 1801 it had caused conflict between king and Parliament, and had resulted in the resignation of Prime Minister Pitt in March of that year.

In 1807, Fuller, in true Tory defence of the established church, was, as ever, highly suspicious of Catholic participation of any form. 'I care no more for a Catholic than I do for a Chinese,' he declared. He countered Sergison with a barrage of campaign posters which bluntly stated his 'No Popery' stance.

He also defended his support of slavery in a poster entitled 'A plain Statement of the Question', in which he stated that he felt the immediate abolition of slavery would mean the loss of England's West Indian colonies 'without which Old England must sink under the burthens of Taxation, and its Navy must be ruined'. He asserted that meddling with the colonies would send England down the same path as revolutionary France and cause the breakdown of the monarchy.

He went on to say that he was not alone in the way he felt and quoted the support of other leading men of the time such as Lord Sidmouth and Lord St Vincent, who had 'voted as he did', and in true politician-style he attempted to take the sting out of the situation and swing opinion his way by declaring he was 'a Friend to gradual Abolition, for he detested Slavery as much as any Man'.

Both these election issues were equally unpopular with Sussex voters. The battle lines were drawn. The fight was on!

    The poll was held in May, 1807, at Lewes and spread over 15 days to enable voters to travel. It also gave the candidates the opportunity of continuing their electioneering during the poll. The method of voting at elections was far different than any electoral procedure we know today. A large platform would normally be erected in the centre of the village or town and the voter, with no privacy whatsoever, would climb the steps, sign his name in the polling book and the officer or sheriff in charge would announce to the crowd which way the person had voted.

Hogarth's painting, 'The Election' perfectly illustrates the disorder surrounding a village polling station

The scene was usually accompanied by disorder and drunkenness and there was much corruption as candidates attempted to bribe the electorate. Voters were often expected simply to sell their vote to the highest bidder — and Fuller was very rich!

As there was no secrecy about the vote there was no way the voter could renege on the deal and it was a brave (or foolish) man who changed his mind and voted the opposite way.

Many voters claimed travelling expenses from the candidates

63

themselves. There was much argument over the amount of expenses paid and Fuller was accused by his opponent of trying to buy his seat. Perhaps Sergison had a valid point. Maybe John Fuller's much-acclaimed honesty was relaxed during the 1807 General Election!

To be fair, it must be pointed out that Fuller was no more a blackguard than anyone else. These were accepted practices in Georgian times and, rightly or wrongly, he was merely following the rules of engagement — and was wealthy enough to indulge. In 1806 Fuller had spoken in Parliament on this very subject, when he strongly defended the practice of paying travelling expenses to voters who had long distances to travel. He declared that no man deserved to be a representative of the people who would not defray the travelling expenses of those who came to support him. He argued that 'such persons, unable to defray the expense of the journey, would simply forfeit their votes' and he concluded 'it would be cruel then to dash this trivial cup from the poor man's lips'.

Preserved in the East Sussex Records Office are many of the bills which were sent to the candidates, in which claims were made for such travelling expenses. A typical example was Thomas Joiner of Fittleworth, who claimed £1.1.0 from Fuller 'for going to Lewes four days and walking back because there was no chaise'. Even food and accommodation taken at inns across the county were claimed for. Exactly how much Fuller spent on his election campaign is not clear, but it is believed to have been a sizeable sum. The diarist, Joseph Farington, 'supposed' the contest cost each candidate £10,000 or £12,000 and another report states that Fuller spent a contributed purse of £30,000 to secure his seat.

At the end of the Lewes election the final count read as follows: Fuller 2530 votes, Sergison 2478. Fuller's margin was a mere 52 votes.

Sergison was not prepared to let the matter rest there. Owing to the closeness of the vote and the suspicion he had about the local sheriff's support for Fuller (yet more bribery?), he petitioned Parliament, complaining of the level of corruption perpetrated by Fuller during the campaign.

However, his protests proved unfruitful and Fuller retained his seat for the next session of Parliament in June 1807.

The year 1807 was to mark the start of a downward slope in Fuller's parliamentary career, as his unbending support for the royal family and a deep rooted concern that plots (imagined or otherwise) were being hatched against his beloved country, would culminate in humiliation and disgrace.

MISGUIDED LOYALTY

On May 30, 1808, John Fuller sought leave to introduce a Parliamentary Bill to prevent the spread of smallpox. Smallpox was one of the biggest worldwide killers in Georgian times. The earlier Fullers themselves had lost a member of the family in 1737, when Hans Fuller (John's uncle), had fallen victim to the disease in Portugal.

The need to isolate patients was considered a necessary precaution and Fuller's proposed Bill suggested that no treatment house for smallpox patients should be placed within a three mile radius of any town, village or assembly and that patients should be kept indoors.

With this and other matters, Fuller continued to play a constructive part in the affairs of Parliament and although a colourful character and certainly no 'shrinking violet', always managed to avoid controversy to any great degree in his earlier years in the House. Apart from the odd outburst over matters such as the slave trade, his behaviour was generally considered to be good.

However, the years 1809 and 1810 were to be quite different and undoubtedly proved to be the most tempestuous period of his political life and it is in these years that we see his name more frequently mentioned in the debates and journals of the House of Commons. His increasingly outspoken views, coupled to a more aggressive attitude, were to lose him friends and eventually land him in deep trouble.

The first episode to throw Fuller into a less than flattering limelight revolved around his overly eager, and somewhat misguided, support for the royal family.

Fuller was a king's man through and through. He never ceased praising his monarch. In a speech in Parliament on March 25, 1807 he grouped the king with Nelson and Pitt when he declared that their names 'ought to be engraven on the hearts of all Englishmen, for the noble services they had rendered to their country; for having in fact been the saviours of our glorious constitution'.

Fuller had every reason to be proud of his king. He was a good man. George III, despite his earlier failings and deteriorating health, had become a well respected monarch. He was deeply religious and his morals were above reproach. He had remained faithful to his wife, Queen Caroline, throughout their long marriage, which had produced 15 children.

Sadly for the king (and the country), his fidelity and moral ideals did not extend to his offspring. The personal failings of his sons contrasted starkly with his own high principles and was bringing the monarchy to its lowest level of public esteem for many years. Indeed there were some who believed the behaviour of the king's sons would result in the very demise of the monarchy.

Known as the 'damndest dukes', they strutted arrogantly through life, indulging in numerous acts of vulgarity, sadism, sexual affairs and the running up of enormous debts to the country. Their deeds were a catalogue of greed, infidelity, selfishness and ingratitude, which caused much embarrassment and distancing from their father.

It must have provided Fuller with a real dilemma. Ardent royalist that he was, even he must have found it hard to justify his support of such people. But support them he did. Many in Parliament did not share his views. They were sickened by the burden the dukes were placing on the country and were ever vigilant to find any excuse to bring them to order.

Such an occurrence happened in 1809, when Parliament found cause to enquire into the underhand dealings of one of the mistresses of Frederick, the Duke of York. Fuller was to become embroiled in much heated debate.

Frederick was the second and favourite son of George III. He was the only one who appeared to gain any respect at all from his father, which made the king's position even more embarrassing. The populace merely tolerated the Duke as an inoffensive but ridiculous buffoon. His marriage to Princess Frederica of Prussia had failed. Incapable of producing children the couple had split.

The Duke embarked on a series of affairs until he eventually settled down in 1804 with Mrs Mary Anne Clarke. He was 40 years old at the time and had recently been promoted to the post of Commander-in-Chief of the British Army, a position he filled with alarming incompe-

tence, best remembered in the following rhyme, inspired by his ill-fated and wasteful deployment of troops in Europe:
The Grand old Duke of York
He had ten thousand men
He marched them up to the top of the hill
And marched them down again.

Mrs Clarke was an attractive 30-year-old, the daughter of a London bricklayer. She had a witty and amusing manner, which much appealed to the Duke. He allowed her £1000 a year and gave her a London home in Gloucester Place with all the trimmings; 20 servants, three cooks and three carriages to get her about.

However, this was not enough for the enterprising Mrs Clarke. She was determined to make more of her opportunities and decided to make hay while the sun shone and before the Duke tired of her. She further feathered her nest by accepting large sums of money in bribes from officers, who knowing of her liaison with the Duke, sought commissions in the army.

Soon the scandal broke and the embarrassed Duke quickly unloaded Mrs Clarke and denied all knowledge of the affair. But that was not the end of it.

On January 27, 1809 the matter was raised in Parliament by a Colonel Wardle who accused the Duke of taking bribes. The motion for an enquiry was seconded by the Member Burdett and a select committee was set up to investigate the charges. Mrs Clarke was among those called to give evidence.

On February 1 she stood before the Bar of the House of Commons and was questioned for two hours about her involvement. In the totally male domain of the House of Commons, Mrs Clarke decided to enjoy her moment of glory. Dressed to kill, she cleverly manipulated the proceedings, delighting many of the Members with her impudent, cheeky manner. At times she had the House in stitches of raucous laughter. She was totally in command, as she pushed the Duke further and further into the mire with every sentence she uttered.

One Member she did not amuse was John Fuller. His face must have grown redder and his temper become more frayed the longer proceedings continued. Infuriated with her flippancy, he considered that the committee 'ought not to proceed with this silly and foolish enquiry'.

At the end of the inquiry nothing could be proved against the Duke, but he had the sense to resign his command of the army before he was pushed. His father reluctantly accepted the resignation and refused to

A PRIVATE EXAMINATION.

doubt for one moment the Duke of York's perfect integrity and his conscientious attention to his public duty.

Public opinion was outraged over the Duke's behaviour. His effigy was burned in the street. Love letters sent to Mrs Clarke were read out in Parliament and the Duke became even more the laughing stock of the nation. Whenever a coin was tossed, it was no longer 'heads or tails' but 'Duke or Darling'.

After the commotion had died down, Mrs Clarke walked away from the affair, perhaps a little tarnished, but unbowed and certainly a good deal wealthier.

Fuller was fuming over her behaviour. On February 3, he forcibly delivered his opinion on the matter by describing the events as 'the foulest conspiracy that ever was set on foot against the son of the Crown and indirectly against the Crown itself' and that 'the Chancellor of the Exchequer had proved, that the Duke of York had, during the space of two years and a half, spent sixteen thousand pounds upon a profligate baggage, and if that would not satisfy the House and the people, he did not know what would'. In his opinion he considered the Duke of York to be a fine military man who had been wrongly maligned.

'A Private Examination', published on March 1 1809. John Fuller is seen on the left emerging from the rays of truth with his Rose Hill bellows

It would appear that Fuller's relationship with the House began to take a turn for the worse during this affair as he challenged the authority of the Speaker (an even more cardinal sin in Georgian times than today). During his boisterous protestations Fuller was called to order, at which he yelled back: 'Why am I out of order?'

The repercussions of the Duke of York/Mrs Clarke affair rumbled on for several months. Fuller received letters of abuse from all quarters, attacking his defence of the Duke. He made enemies in the House. He attacked the original sponsors of the motion and their supporters Whitbread and Folkestone. He termed them 'a fraction to overturn Royalty' and said that if they didn't like living in England, 'Damn 'em, leave it.' The remarks caused great offence and uproar in the House.

The Duke of York/Mrs Clarke affair was extremely popular and provided juicy copy for the cartoonists and satirists of the time. Nearly 200 prints caricaturing the scandal were produced and can be found in the Catalogue of Political and Personal Prints in The British Museum. Fuller features prominently in two of them.

In 'A Private Examination', published on March 1 1809, all the leading players are portrayed. Fuller is seen emerging from the rays of truth, blasting the lady with his Rose Hill Bellows as he roars at her: 'I'll blast her no Forging here you baggage. And still I blew a Fuller blast. And gave a lustier cheer.'

Another print is entitled 'Whitewashing a Darling at the Original Whitewashing Shop or how to make a Black General White.' The black Duke of York is shown being whitewashed clean. The comments Fuller made in the House are reproduced.

As a footnote to the story, it would appear the Duke did regain some confidence, when he was eventually reinstated to his position as head of the armed forces by his brother, the Prince Regent in 1811 and he served in the post until his death in 1827. His statue can be seen today overlooking The Mall in Waterloo Place. It is 124ft from base to head, of a sufficient height, so it was suggested, to keep the Duke out of the way of his creditors. When he died his debts amounted to a staggering £2 million. The cost of the statue was met by stopping one day's pay from every soldier in the army. The column was designed by Benjamin Wyatt and is of the Tuscan order. Above its capital there is a square balcony, a drum and a dome. The bronze statue is by Sir Richard Westmacott.

WHITEWASHING a DARLING at the Original Whitewashing Shop or how to make a Black General White

DISGRACE

After his involvement in the Duke of York/Mrs Clarke scandal, there was worse to come for John Fuller. The following year he would have his own scandal, which would lead to complete disgrace.

The most frequently-quoted remark attributed to Fuller's later political days was that he called the Speaker 'an insignificant little man in the wig'.

There are several colourful versions of the incident. An account by Hilaire Belloc in his book, *The Four Men*, tells of Fuller leaping to his feet during a particularly dull debate and, much to the dismay of the House, delivering in his booming voice, a glowing account of the virtues of living in his much-loved Sussex. After defying the cries of 'Order, Order' for several minutes, and with the House in total uproar, the Speaker called for him to cease, at which Fuller bellowed: 'Do you think that I care for you, you insignificant man in the wig? Take that!' and then left the totally bewildered House to return to Brightling.

Stirring stuff, but almost certainly riddled with poetic licence. Belloc's *The Four Men* was written in 1902 and the book is a chronicle of the beauty of Sussex and the strength of its characters, and it would have been most tempting for him to use Jack Fuller as the mouthpiece for extolling the virtues of the county.

According to M Lower in *The Book of Sussex Worthies* Fuller was publicly reprimanded when, in 1810, he swore at the Speaker during a debate on the slave issue in the House of Commons, when 'he gave utterance to language in that august assembly which his warmest friends could but condemn'. It would appear that this version of the story is also flawed, for although ever ready to defend the slave trade, sometimes most forcibly, there is no evidence to suggest Fuller overstepped the mark or showed any disrespect for the Speaker when speaking on the subject in the House.

To find the truth of the matter, it is necessary to consult the Journal of the House of Commons, where the entry for February 27, 1810 is most enlightening. It clearly shows that Fuller badly disgraced himself in the House that day.

He was serving on a committee which was enquiring into the reasons behind a disastrous military expedition to Holland the previous July. A force of 40,000 men had been sent to Walcheren with three objectives; firstly to divert French troops northwards, secondly to destroy Napoleon's naval base at Antwerp and lastly to raise a Dutch revolt. All three objectives failed. The Earl of Chatham was in command and he dallied in Flushing for over a month, so that the French were given time to fortify Antwerp. The whole project resulted in disaster when they had to evacuate Walcheren, leaving a garrison of 15,000 men, 7,000 perishing from malaria and 3,000 being permanently incapacitated. The loss was compounded by the Government's failure to insist on prompt withdrawal.

Fuller, his patriotic fervour running high, suspected a plot against king and country and began to talk out of turn, the volume and tone of his language becoming more bitter as the debate progressed.

The Journal for February 27, 1810 tells us that 'a Member of the Committee had misbehaved himself during the Sitting of the Committee, making use of profane oaths, and disturbing their Proceedings; John Fuller Esquire, Member for Sussex, the Member complained of, was heard to excuse himself; in the doing of which he gave greater offence, by repeating and persisting in his disorderly conduct'.

The Speaker then called Fuller by his name and demanded his withdrawal from the chamber and for him to be placed in custody. The Serjeant at Arms was called to ensure Fuller complied.

The House then resumed with its business. But Fuller was raging. He still had more to say. He burst free of the Serjeant at Arms and stormed back into the House, 'in a very violent and disorderly manner' hurling insults at all and sundry and generally causing a great commotion. The Journal goes on: 'Mr Speaker resumed the Chair, and ordered the Serjeant to do his duty; Mr Fuller was accordingly taken out by the Serjeant, assisted by his Messengers'. The rampant Fuller was placed in the prison rooms, which were situated in the Palace Yard at Westminster and left to cool off.

The following day he was full of remorse for his deeds. The Journal stated: 'A Member in his place, having informed the House, that Mr Fuller had requested him to offer his excuse to the House for his misbehaviour. And a Motion being made, and the Question being put, That John Fuller Esquire be discharged; it passed in the negative.'

On Thursday March 1, a short debate took place in the House on the action to be taken against him. The first speaker was the Chancellor of the Exchequer, who stated that although he recognised the seriousness of the 'disagreeable occurrence' he considered that, as Fuller had made apologies for his actions, he should be 'discharged out of custody'.

But not all felt the same way. Earl Temple, along with other Members, strongly opposed the proposal and thought Fuller should receive a more severe reprimand. He described the incident as 'an extraordinary, outrageous and highly aggravated insult which had been experienced by the House: an outrage the more serious as it had been committed within their walls; and the more aggravated as it had been directed, not to the Members alone, but to the person of the Speaker'.

Although vague as to what exactly Fuller said in his outburst, it must have been pretty bad. Reaction from other Members of the House bore this out. Terms such as 'Mad Bull' were thrown at Fuller. Mr Whitbread, his old adversary from the Duke of York/Mrs Clarke affair, said he 'had never witnessed such a gross outrage' in 20 years at the House and suggested that but for 'an accidental circumstance' the outrage had been prevented from proceeding to the utmost violence. What the 'accidental circumstance' was is not recorded.

Whitbread, who must have quietly enjoyed Fuller's predicament, suggested that not only should Fuller be discharged from the House of Commons but that he should be sent to Newgate Gaol or even the Tower of London.

One theory to explain Fuller's behaviour is that he may have been under the influence of alcohol. Was this what one Member of the House was hinting at during the debate, when he stated that 'he believed it to be admitted, that the hon member (Fuller) was then in a situation in which he could not altogether appreciate the very improper nature of his conduct?' Joseph Farington was under the same impression. He stated in his entry for March 1 that Fuller's outrageous behaviour was due to 'the effect of intoxication'.

After several more Members had voiced their opinion in the debate, an amendment was passed 'that Mr Fuller be brought to the bar to apologise to the House, and that if the apology should be deemed sufficient, he might be discharged'.

Fuller was then brought before the House, where he received a

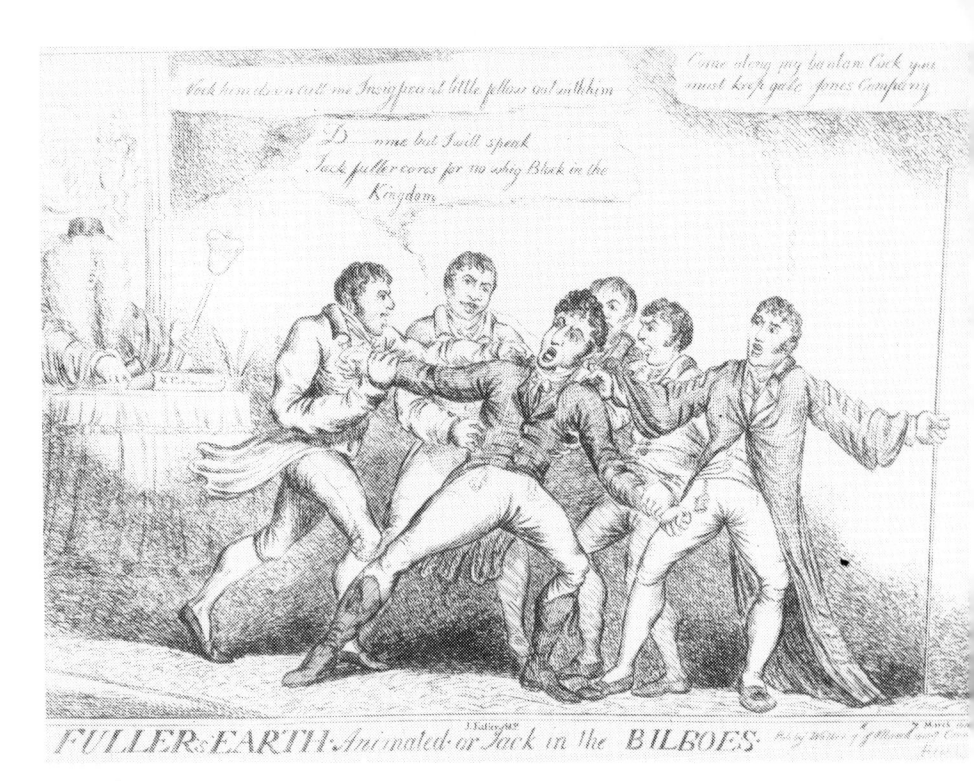

Fuller is ejected from the House of Commons. The artist has been somewhat flattering to him. By this stage of his career he would almost certainly have sported a larger, more rounded figure

severe reprimand from the Speaker. He was also ordered to pay a fine. The Speaker's words were duly entered in the Journals of the House.

Fuller, realising he had overstepped the mark, showed great remorse for his outburst, and offered an unconditional apology, which was accepted and he was released from custody that day.

Had these ample apologies not been forthcoming, it is believed his punishment would have been far less lenient. Another factor must have been his previously good behaviour. Even Fuller's fellow Tories expressed embarrassment at his outburst.

For his pains Fuller gained the dubious honour of being featured in his own caricature, published on March 7, 1810. Entitled 'Fuller's Earth Animated or Jack in the Bilboes', it shows Fuller being removed from the House by the Serjeant at Arms and his four attendants. The Speaker is seen shouting: 'Nock him down call me Insignificant little fellow out with him'. This cartoon could well have been the source of Hilaire Belloc's colourful version of events.

As a footnote to the story of the failed Walcheren expedition, it would appear that it was not only John Fuller's feelings which were stirred to boiling point. The episode resulted in the loss of two prominent members of the Cabinet of the day.

The Secretary for War, Lord Castlereagh, so incensed by the Foreign Secretary Canning's criticism of his handling of the affair, challenged him to a duel with pistols on Putney Heath. Both men missed with their first shots but with their second, Canning hit Castlereagh in the chest and Castlereagh (considered an expert shot), hit Canning in the thigh. Both of them then retired from public affairs to recover from their injuries. Yet another example of the crazy world of Georgian politics!

As far as Fuller was concerned his scandal in the House had severely dented his reputation as a Member and after 1810 his enthusiasm for Parliament appeared to decline. A less intense Fuller would now attend the House of Commons. In March 1810 he wrote to his cousin John Trayton Fuller in subdued mood: 'I shall go down to Parliament today having in some measure recovered my temper.' The Walcheren episode was still on his mind. He complained that a question he had put to Lord Saltern during the heated debate regarding the British Navy's support during the ill-fated expedition had not been entered in the Minutes of Evidence. He felt aggrieved but realised that having disgraced himself and narrowly escaped a long prison sentence, he must bite his tongue. At a later date, when he had fully regained his composure, a reflective Fuller referred to his brush with the Speaker as a 'nonsensical dispute.'

However, the Walcheren incident did not deflate him totally and we still see his name cropping up in later debates on issues close to his heart.

In November 1810, the subject under debate in the House was the state of the king's health. Since 1788, the king had intermittently suffered from incapacitating fits that gave the appearance of progressively worsening mental illness.

In 1810 he suffered a relapse which left him permanently deranged and blind. It was generally accepted that the king was mad and his capacity to rule was in serious doubt.

At the end of 1810, Parliament was discussing the implications of his son, Prince George becoming Regent and standing in for the ailing king.

Fuller found the idea unappealing. He suggested to the House they should resist such a step and reasoned that 'there is every probability of his perfect restoration to sanity of mind and body. What would we have more?'. He went on to ask: 'Will any in this House be base enough to desert our poor, good old man, in his adversity? Whoever deserts the dear old king is the basest of human beings, of human creatures; I care not whether he be prince or peasant; be him prince or peasant than rats, I say, blow him from this earth!'

Unfortunately for Fuller, the king did not recover and the following year Prince George took over as Regent till his father's death in 1820.

Poor King George III has entered the history books, quite unfairly, as the 'mad king'. By studying the reports of his physicians, modern doctors have since established that he was suffering from a hereditary physical illness known as porphyria.

In 1812, the last of Fuller's years in political life, Parliament was stunned by an appalling act of violence, when the serving Prime Minister, Spencer Perceval was gunned down by a madman as he was about to enter the House. At a later date, a sombre Fuller rose in the House to suggest that some form of monument be erected to the late Prime Minister's memory and that the sum of 4000 guineas be put aside for the purpose. The result, the work of Joseph Nollekens, can be seen today in Westminster Abbey.

John Fuller did not seek re-election for the next Parliamentary term. Perhaps, due to his disgrace in the House two years earlier, he sensed a falling off in support and was not prepared to risk failure in any future election — or maybe he had just had enough. Whatever the reasons, his political career was over.

King George III, a long-serving and popular monarch

1812 OVERTURES

In the month of September 1812, the Parliamentary session was dissolved. John Fuller would have no further part to play. He had made his intentions known and the Sussex 'interests' were thrown into confusion as they turned their thoughts towards selecting a replacement.

Fuller's decision to quit prompted the start of a frantic session of letter-writing between the prominent men of the county. Feelings seemed to be mixed over Fuller's departure from the political scene. Many disliked him, but it would appear he was a hard act to follow and the general attitude was 'better the devil you know'. Several other suggestions regarding a replacement were put forward. Lord Ashburnham was approached to stand, but declined. The 'interests' then turned their attention to his son. Lord Ashburnham, in a letter to Lord Chichester said he was reluctant to have his son represent the county and suggested that Fuller might still be persuaded to stand again. 'I suspect that he would not be deaf to the voice of the county if it should be once more rais'd to call upon to come forward.'

Lord Sheffield was certainly not keen on Fuller returning to Parliament. He claimed it would be 'direfull work to support Fuller, who has hardly a well-wisher', but he was still confused as to who should take his place. He concluded his letter: 'In short we are in a strange state.'

Fuller received a visit from the Earl of Chichester, who asked him to reconsider his resignation. He also suggested that if Fuller was adamant on leaving the House, then his nephew, Augustus Elliot Fuller, should be put forward in his place. In a letter to Lord Chichester, dated the following day, Fuller reiterated his intention to quit, stating that he considered he had more than done his duty. It would appear from this letter there had been some kind of family rift. Fuller found the suggestion that his nephew's nomination was quite unacceptable as he claimed that Augustus' father, John Trayton Fuller, once a great friend and fellow cavalry officer, had swindled him out of a share of an estate in Kent and he felt the offspring of such a man would not be an appropriate choice for Parliament.

This rift between Fuller and his family is mentioned in several of the letters, which continued to be exchanged at a more and more frantic pace. Many of the comments in them were far from complimentary to Fuller. Chichester referred to Fuller's 'indecisive wavering' and outrageous conduct at the 1807 General Election. There were carping references to his vanity and in one correspondence he was irreverently referred to as 'Blast'. Egremont suggested it would be 'so much the better if we can get another and have his interest'. But Egremont was unable to offer any suggestions. He was also experiencing selection problems, due to his brother's inability through illness, to stand again for the west of the county. Eventually it was decided that Walter Burrell, Esq of West Grinstead Park should stand for West Sussex and Egremont hoped the situation in the east would soon be resolved.

After exploring the suitability of several other possible candidates, Sir Godfrey Webster, flamboyant owner of the Battle Abbey estate, emerged as the frontrunner. He had received a letter from his friend Fuller declaring his support. Business and sporting connections between the Fuller and Webster families had existed for many years and John Fuller and Sir Godfrey were well acquainted through their shared interest in fox hunting. Fuller thought Sir Godfrey well suited to serve the county. Sir Godfrey had also received the backing of Glenbervie of Battle, who considered him 'very well looking, very good-natured and gentlemanlike'.

Sir Godfrey Webster was eventually elected to the House of Commons in 1812 and served as Member for Sussex County until 1820.

Augustus Elliot Fuller's rift with his uncle must have eventually been healed. He inherited the Sussex estates from him in 1834 and did eventually get the opportunity to serve as Member for the county from 1841 till his death in 1857.

The Parliamentary scene had lost its interest for John Fuller in 1812. There were other things to concentrate on and a very different side of his character had emerged.

A GEORGIAN PHARAOH

It would appear that the incident in the House of Commons in the February of 1810 had a most profound effect on John Fuller. At the still relatively young age of 53, different aspects of his character began to emerge; a more mellow and caring attitude developed as he became less interested in parliamentary affairs. His political career had become severely undermined by self-destructive actions, but destiny was to take a change of course. He adopted a more relaxed, less troubled approach to life as he become a patron of the arts and sciences and became more intent on using his great wealth for the benefit of others. It was also around this time he initiated the building of his unusual structures.

But there were also strange, contrasting thoughts in Fuller's mind. In 1810, in the true style of the Egyptian Pharaohs, he was preparing for death. Soon after his disgrace in the House of Commons, he approached the Rector of Brightling Church with an unusual request. The Rector's response can be found in the Burials and Baptism Register of Brightling Parish where the following entry, dated November 15, 1810, is scribbled in the margin:

'Be it remembered that John Fuller Esq of Rose Hill at the beginning of the present year applied for permission to erect a mausoleum in Brightling Churchyard and to lay open the south side of the said churchyard by removing the old Post and rail fence and erecting a stonewall: and when he had fixed upon the site for erecting his Edifice he inquired of me as Incumbent of the Living what would satisfy me for the ground it was to stand on: my reply was that as he would be at a considerable expense in erecting the wall which would be a good improvement I should not demand any fee for the other building. The wall is now finished and John Fuller Esq had added thereto a couple of substantial stone pillars and an iron gate way. The testor J.B. Hayley, Rector.'

In the 'Faculty for a Mausoleum in the Churchyard of the Parish Church of Brightling in the County of Sussex for John Fuller Esq', dated June 15, 1811, the Bishop of Chichester stated that John Fuller 'had erected and built in the Churchyard of the Parish Church of Brightling aforesaid a Mausoleum Sepulchre or Burying Place for himself, his heirs, family and friends in the South East side of the Churchyard'.

So the deal was completed. The Rector got his wall and new gate and Fuller gained his tomb. It is interesting to reflect on the reaction of the Rector when Mr Fuller's mausoleum finally took shape. Could he ever have anticipated the gigantic size of the structure when he granted his consent?

It would be a further 24 years before Fuller would finally enter his tomb and those years were to be crammed with good deeds as he gained recognition and distinction as a great philanthropist and benefactor to his fellow men.

And, of course, there were the follies.

PAINT ME FINE PICTURES

During his years in public life, Fuller had made the acquaintance of many people in the world of the arts. They included the writer Sir Walter Scott, painter Henry Singleton, sculptors Sir Francis Chantry, Joseph Nollekens and Peter Rouw and the composer William Shield.

Indeed, in the time of George III, many men of substance had become more appreciative of art in all its forms. But in Fuller's case, after his disgrace in the House of Commons, he certainly seemed more determined than most to gain solace in the world of culture. His wealth enabled him to surround himself with men of the highest calibre. Nothing but the best would do for Mr Fuller!

Undoubtedly the most famous of his acquaintances was the painter J M W Turner. From 1790 till 1840, in an increasingly mechanised world, British art was dominated by the Romantic movement and Turner was one of its greatest exponents. His huge painted canvases displayed a unique combination of nature and drama. The gentleness and softness of his pictures and his atmospheric use of space and colour gave pleasure to many — and still do.

It is not clear how Fuller first met this colossus of English art, but it is most likely the two men were introduced by the 3rd Earl of Egremont at his Petworth estate in West Sussex. Fuller and Egremont had become acquainted through their involvement with the Sussex Volunteer Yeomanry Troops and Fuller would probably have been a regular visitor to Petworth.

Egremont had known Turner since 1802 and had commissioned him to paint views of his estate at Petworth House. He was a great patron of the artist and they had become friends. It is most probable that Fuller

'Battle Abbey, the spot where Harold fell', used in 'Views of Sussex', published in 1820

was invited to Petworth to view Turner's work and was so impressed by what he saw, he asked Turner to visit Rose Hill.

Whatever the circumstances of their meeting, Joseph Farington wrote on April 21, 1810:

> 'Mr Fuller, Member for Suffolk has engaged Turner to go into that county to make drawings of three or four views. He is to have 100 gns for the *use* of his drawings, which are to be returned to him.'

Apart from naming the wrong county, the diary entry seems quite accurate. Turner and Fuller got on very well together and Turner was a guest at Rose Hill for much of the year, during which time he made a number of sketches, from which he later painted four Sussex watercolours and an oil painting of Rose Hill. Fuller hired the drawings for 100 guineas and had them made into prints to circulate among his gentry friends. Eventually he bought all four watercolours from Turner.

It was a tremendous coup by Fuller to have gained the services of such an outstanding talent. It certainly reflects his great wealth. Turner was 35 years of age at the time of his first visit to Rose Hill and was already an established and wealthy man, whose paintings sold well at very high prices.

This rather destroys the often mooted theory that Fuller was one of

Turner's first major sponsors and had helped a struggling artist to make his name. By the time of his meeting with Fuller, Turner had already accumulated a considerable fortune.

His rise to fame had been swift. Born in humble surroundings in 1775, at Maiden Lane, off the Strand, Joseph Mallord William Turner was the son of a barber. He started his career as a topographical draughtsman but by 1802 had become a member of the Royal Academy and later opened his own gallery in Harley Street. He became Professor of Perspective at the Royal Academy in 1808, a position he held till 1838.

As well as the commissioned work, Fuller started a collection of the great artist's paintings, especially those of Sussex. In all Fuller eventually owned 13 Turner watercolours and two oil paintings. They were proudly displayed at Rose Hill and his Devonshire Place home. They had cost him a huge sum. In Turner's account books there are three entries for the year 1810 against Fuller's name, which totalled £617 16s 3d and the following year a further £417 was entered. And there was much more to follow.

In 1815 Turner painted a fine view of Rose Hill, which can be seen today at the British Museum. It was also in this year that Fuller financed the line-engraving of several Sussex scenes he had purchased from Turner. The first part of this project was published in 1820 under the

Another engraving from 'Views in Sussex': 'Brightling Observatory from Rose Hill Park'

title 'Views of Sussex'. The five engravings were: 'Brightling Observatory from Rose Hill Park', 'The Vale of Ashburnham', 'Pevensey Bay from Crowhurst Park', 'Battle Abbey' and 'The Vale of Heathfield'. It was planned there would be two more parts to the series but, for various reasons, they did not come to fruition. It is said Fuller wanted the views for his projected 'History of East Sussex', the publication of which, unfortunately, did not materialise. What an interesting book that would have been!

Turner was at Rose Hill on and off from 1810 till 1818. In 1819 he visited Venice, a trip which was to have a profound effect on his later work. Towards the end of his life Turner suffered ill health and he died, a bachelor, at Chelsea in 1851. He was buried with full honours in St Paul's Cathedral.

In his later life Turner held strong anti-slavery feelings, but one must assume that at the time of his initial meeting with Fuller, these had not surfaced. If they had, Turner must surely have bitten his tongue in pursuance of the lucrative commission offered by Fuller.

There is an amusing story about Turner's association with Fuller worth mentioning. It would appear that Turner also had a touch of eccentricity about him. (Is this why they got on so well?) Although he showed great generosity to his fellow artists, it seems this good will did not extend to his clients.

When Turner had completed his original painting of Rose Hill in 1810, he was invited to Fuller's Devonshire Place residence where a cheque was handed to him for his work. After breakfasting, he thanked Fuller and left. About five minutes later there was a knock on the door. The wealthy artist had returned to claim his three shillings fare for his hackney carriage. Fuller laughed loudly as he paid up.

It was a story he always enjoyed relating to his friends.

Detail from the cover of
'Views of Sussex'

IN SEARCH OF IMPROVEMENTS

The 18th century and early 19th century were in many respects the halcyon periods of the British landed classes. Bolstered by political power and increased revenue from their estates, attention was turned to the improvement of their dwellings.

There was much interest in continental architecture. The English country house was the focal point of the estate and the so-called leaders of society took their inspiration from the sights and experiences gained from their tours to the continent of Europe.

Many wealthy young men in the 18th century embarked on what became known as The Grand Tour. Journeys were undertaken to the great European centres of art and learning such as Paris and Venice and later to the glories of Athens and Rome. Although it could sometimes be a dangerous adventure with the threat of robbery or death on mountainous roads, The Grand Tour was considered an essential ingredient in a young gentleman's education.

They were greatly influenced by classical architecture and returned to Britain to transform their homes. The upper classes of the period saw themselves as the inheritors of the traditions of ancient Roman (and later Greek) antiquity and travellers brought back cultural inspirations of all kinds from their journeys. It was a frantic age for architectural experiment based on continental themes and few towns in Britain today are without some trace of the impact of Italian or Greek historic architecture.

It is recorded that earlier members of the Fuller family experienced the delights of foreign travel. Documents in the East Sussex Records Office tell us that in 1731 the first John Fuller of Brightling (Jack's grandfather) sailed with members of his family to Calais, where they were met by his son Rose, who escorted them to Paris. They later travelled through France and Flanders. John Fuller described them as 'the finest countries I ever saw'.

Whether Jack Fuller actually embarked on such a continental tour is not known, but he certainly seemed determined to enter into the spirit of the age. For it was in 1810 his thoughts turned to his building projects.

The comings and goings of important visitors to Rose Hill in the year 1810 were most significant. As soon as Turner had completed his work, Fuller took steps to enlist the services of a man who had widely travelled the continent and who would eventually become one of the most famous architects in the country.

The entry for July 29, 1810 in Joseph Farington's diary, reads: 'Robt. Smirke went today to Rose Hill, Mr Fullers.'

Robert Smirke, RA FSA FRS Hons FRIBA (1780-1867) was regarded as the leading exponent of the Greek Revival period, when emphasis was shifted from Roman architecture. He was a pupil of Sir John Soane and was greatly influenced by the work of George Dance Jr. He travelled extensively in Italy and Greece between 1801 and 1805 and a year later published a work entitled 'Specimens of Continental Architecture'.

As with Turner, it is not fully documented how Fuller came to know him or where they were introduced. What is known is that Smirke was a friend of Turner and perhaps the painter acted as a middle man in recommending Smirke to Fuller.

It is also not certain exactly why Smirke was called to Rose Hill, but it is believed that he may have been commissioned to advise on alterations to the mansion. There is reference to his work on the grand drawing room of the mansion around this period, when the walls were encased in a facing of Roman cement. This large room was demolished in 1955 and the chimney breast saved and removed. It was sold to Hambros Bank and was until recently displayed at its former London offices.

Perhaps Fuller summoned Smirke, a fellow freemason, to Rose Hill specifically to discuss his folly buildings. A likely supposition is that one project led to the other. The pyramid tomb was built between November 15, 1810 and June 15, 1811 and it is, therefore, reasonable to assume that Smirke had a say in the design of the structure. It is suggested he based it on the Tomb of Cestius in Rome, as he had returned from a trip to Italy in 1805 and was much inspired by what he had seen.

Fuller could certainly afford to pick men of the highest calibre for the work he required. By the time of their meeting Smirke was already climbing the ladder of success and in 1808 his name had shot to prominence when the Covent Garden Theatre was opened — the first Greek Doric building in London.

Later, in 1813 he was to become one of the architects of the Board of Works and at the age of 33, had risen to the pinnacle of his profession and was very much the favoured architect of the Establishment. Many important commissions came his way.

Probably his greatest and most remembered achievement was the building of the façade of The British Museum between 1823 and 1827. He designed many other famous buildings in London including Somerset House, The Royal Mint and the General Post Office. He was knighted in 1832.

His involvement with the buildings at Brightling is not fully documented, the Observatory being the only structure for which plans are available, but almost certainly he was responsible for the design of the Rotunda Temple and greatly influenced the design of the Obelisk and, as previously mentioned, the Pyramid, although probably Fuller himself had a far greater say in these.

Sir Robert Smirke and one of his greatest creations, the façade of the British Museum

Before: Humphry Repton's sketch of Rose Hill

The improvement of a gentleman's property in the 18th century nearly always extended to the land surrounding his great house and the period became renowned for the laying out of grounds and the emergence of many well-known landscape gardeners.

Around 1730, William Kent became the first true master of the art. With rolling lawns close to the house and the careful positioning of distant trees, glades and architectural eyecatchers, his objective was to form a pleasurable and surprising aspect for his clients.

Kent's style was enthusiastically followed by many imitators, none more successfully than Lancelot (Capability) Brown. His nickname was derived from his ability to assess an area's potential and his skill in bringing his ideas to fruition. Born in 1716, Brown set up business in 1751 and during his lifetime created over 200 landscape gardens across the country, including the magnificent examples at Blenheim Palace in Oxfordshire and Sheffield Park in Sussex.

The landscaping of Brightling Park points very much to his style, although it is believed that not all of his suggestions were implemented. The work was instigated during the years of Rose Fuller's occupancy in 1763, when Brown was regarded as the leading improver of grounds in

After: The same viewpoint, but this time Repton's proposed alterations are shown

the country. Around this time he was also responsible for the laying out of Ashburnham Park, only five miles from Brightling.

There was also a family connection. Jack Fuller's sister, Frances, married Brown's son, Lancelot and although this was after Capability Brown's death in 1783, it can reasonably be assumed the families were previously acquainted.

The plan for Rose Hill is mentioned in correspondence between Jack Fuller and one of Brown's greatest admirers and undisputed successor, Humphry Repton, who visited Rose Hill several times during 1806. Fuller had sought his advice on making alterations to the house and grounds and Repton made his first visit to survey the area 'in a deep snow' on March 12.

In June 1806 Repton delivered a comprehensive report on how he thought Rose Hill and its grounds could be improved.

Repton, who sought to bring more colour into his garden designs with additional flowers and terraces, had a stylish way of presenting his recommendations to clients in the form of notes bound in red leather, accompanied by watercolour drawings of the grounds with an attached overlap to show his proposed alterations. He used all his subtle powers of persuasion to cajole wealthy landowners into parting with their money. Some who implemented his suggestions found themselves unable to keep up with the costs and were plunged into financial embarrassment. Repton also played heavily on the vanity of his prospective clients. In Fuller's case he insisted that Rose Hill was not just 'the villa of a citizen, it is the mansion of a British senator, surrounded by his property and by his constituents.'

In the 'Red Book for Rose Hill', now preserved in the Bodleian Library, Oxford, Repton made it clear he was not happy with the siting of the house and suggested an extensive rebuilding programme and sweeping changes to the grounds. He also made uncharacteristically critical comments about 'Mr Brown's plan' for the estate when he stated that although he had 'the most perfect respect for his genius and talents' he considered Brown had mistaken the treatment of Rose Hill, 'by not sufficiently consulting the comfort of habitation, rather than the advantages of beauty in the situation'.

He continued: 'After so frequently admiring and defending Mr Brown's plans for other places, it is with regret that I must condemn that proposed for Rose Hill; which had it been completed, would have sacrificed all comfort to prospect, and for the sake of an extensive view, would have rendered the house almost uninhabitable.' Repton also considered Brown's proposed additions to the south west as 'replete with absurdity'.

Repton made further visits to Rose Hill during October 1806, but his somewhat radical ideas obviously did not meet with Fuller's approval and his recommendations were not executed. A year after his initial visit, Repton reluctantly accepted, in a letter dated March 10, 1807, Fuller's decision not to act on his advice.

Another example of Repton's fanciful plans for Rose Hill

VIOLATION OF PRIVACY

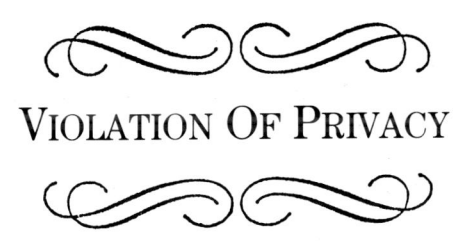

Although the building of the follies at Brightling is hard to date, due to the lack of any accurate documentation, it can reasonably be assumed that they were all completed between the years 1810 and 1820.

The largest building project undertaken by Fuller was the construction of an estate wall to enclose Rose Hill. Surrounding the park and stretching for four miles, the wall varied in height from four to six feet and clearly illustrates Fuller's readiness to provide employment in the hard times following the Napoleonic Wars.

Unemployment was extremely high at the time and with deposed peasant farmers eager to scrape a living and soldiers returning from the wars, there was a surplus of labour in the country areas. These were times of extreme hardship. Unemployment reached its peak in 1817 and it was not until many country workers moved to the industrial towns to seek employment that the situation eased.

Fuller is said to have laid out £10,000 in five to seven years for labour, paying numerous workers half their normal pay — one shilling a day — to build the wall and perform other maintenance duties. The main activity was between 1815 and 1817.

In more recent times the wall had fallen into a much-dilapidated condition, mainly due to the ravages of time and partly due to people helping themselves to stones for their private use. However, through the efforts of the Sussex Historic Gardens Restoration Society, moves were made during 1983 and 1984 to enlist the aid of the Manpower Services Commission, which undertook the task of restoring the wall to its former state. The YMCA was appointed as its agent, and the young people of this organisation, under the initial expert guidance of master mason, Mr Danny Elliott, carried out the actual rebuilding programme. History came full circle with the wall providing much-needed employment, a century and a half later. The spirit of John Fuller lives on.

During the year 1820 Fuller found his wall — and his privacy — had been breached. There were several acts of trespass on his land and over a period of several months gates and stiles were damaged on the western side of his estate.

These deeds had been perpetrated by one individual — John Randoll. Fuller knew who the culprit was and instructed his gamekeeper and eventually his solicitor to instruct Randoll to refrain from his practices.

However, the warnings fell on deaf ears and Randoll continued to trespass, causing still further damage with his dogs. The reasons for Randoll's persistent abuse of Fuller's privacy can only be guessed at. Perhaps he was driven by envy, or maybe he held a grudge against the squire. Eventually Fuller's patience was exhausted and he proceeded to take the offender to court.

The case eventually came before the King's Bench Special Jury in 1822 when Jack Fuller was the plaintiff. There was little defence from Randoll as Fuller easily won and was awarded damages.

The case is documented in the East Sussex Records Office, and the court's pronouncement stated that Mr Fuller's privacy should be respected due to his great service, whereby he had 'laid out at least ten thousand pounds in the employment of the labourers and mechanics of his village who would have otherwise often unemployed'. The court agreed that for these reasons Fuller's 'amusements should not be unreasonably interferred with'.

Randoll was extremely fortunate. Not only had he caused damage, but had shot game while on Fuller's estate and although trespass was serious enough, poaching could be punishable by death.

BEYOND THE CALL OF DUTY

John Fuller's attitude to religion was, like most things in his life, down-to-earth. It would appear he could not stand the over-pious approach of some around him. 'Just as the man who pretends to more courage than another has generally less, so he who pretends to more religion than others, is often the greater cheat.' So said the Squire of Brightling!

Nevertheless, despite his rakish manner and suggested lax morals associated with Georgian landowners, he still deemed it most important for the squire of the village to act as father-figure and to outwardly be seen to be upholding the principles of Christianity by making regular attendance at services and high on his list of responsibilities was the care and maintenance of the village church. The church, along with the public house, was the gathering place for the villagers and in this way contributed to the smooth running of village life.

John Fuller accepted his responsibility with enthusiastic vigour. His support for St Thomas a Becket Church went far beyond the call of duty and his generous donations were numerous. If one could buy a place in Heaven, Fuller must surely be sitting in God's lap!

One of his most spectacular gifts was a barrel organ — the largest in Britain still in full working order — which he donated in 1820, along with the gallery to support it. Fuller commissioned W A A Nichols to make the instrument, which has six stops with two barrels each playing 12 tunes. Until 1920, Herbert Croft and his father, who were local parishioners, played it for voluntaries. It was restored in 1960 and is still played today on special occasions.

When the organ was first installed Fuller presented the male members of the choir with white smocks, buckskin breeches and yellow stockings and the females with red cloaks to be worn on the day the organ was first played and afterwards.

Detail from the bells

In preparation for a visit by the bishop, Fuller refurbished the interior of the church by boxing in and plastering the walls of the nave and chancel and painting them with whitewash. Unfortunately, in his enthusiasm, he painted over some of the extremely rare wall paintings which adorned the church. They were rediscovered in 1966.

In 1815 Fuller paid tribute to his favourite soldier, when he had the five bells in the tower recast and added a new treble which was inscribed: 'The five bells recast and a new treble added at the expense of John Fuller Esq, late Member for this county. Anno Domini 1815. In honour of the illustrious Duke of Wellington, his last six victories are here recorded.'

The other five bells were given the names of Wellington's six battles: Toulouse, Orthes, Pyrenees, Vittoria, Salamanca and Tallavera. Two bells were given in 1818, inscribed 'Waterloo', so making a peal of eight. One of these was inscribed 'This peal of bells was completed Anno Domini 1818 at the expense of John Fuller Esq.'

Standing in the beautiful church today, it is quite easy to imagine John Fuller attending church services, shuffling his huge frame in the family box pew and surveying all before him with an ever-critical eye. The box pew still remains and is today used by the present owners of Brightling Park. On the window behind is the Fuller coat of arms and motto.

To give himself a lasting physical appearance, Fuller instructed that a bust be placed on the wall of the church. It is the work of Sir Francis Chantry and was sculpted in 1819. It shows Fuller in a flattering Romanesque pose — toga and all. Beneath this is a plaque by Henry Rouw with the inscription: 'Utile nihil quod non honestrum' — Nothing is of use which is not honest.

The choice of Chantry to make the bust yet again illustrates how Fuller's great wealth enabled him to employ the very best of craftsmen.

Chantry was the foremost sculptor of his time, much in demand by the rich and famous. Many of his works can be seen in and around London, one of the best known being the equestrian statue of George IV in Trafalgar Square and his most talked of creation is *The Sleeping Children* in Lichfield Cathedral.

But it was Chantry's busts which gained him most praise and recognition. One of the most famous is that of Sir Walter Scott and there is an interesting story which tells how John Fuller influenced the finished product. It had been Chantry's intention to portray Scott in a studiously solemn pose and he invited the writer to breakfast with him and several acquaintances before the sitting. During breakfast Fuller joined the party in typically boisterous cheery mood and was introduced to Sir Walter, who at first eyed him with suspicion. However, after an hour or so of lighthearted chat, with Fuller expounding numerous bawdy tales, Sir Walter took a distinct liking to him.

Chantry had been watching the proceedings carefully and when Scott left after the sitting, the sculptor declared he would abandon the solemn pose he had planned. He made alterations to the face and gave Sir Walter a more relaxed — and happier — countenance. Sir Walter was delighted with the outcome and Fuller added yet another famous name to his list of friends.

There are also two plaques in Brightling Church commemorating Fuller's friends. William Shield, Master of His Majesty's Band of Music,

Sketch of John Fuller by Sir Francis Chantry

Chantry's bust of Fuller in Brightling Church

and Dr Primrose Blair, physician to His Majesty's Fleet in the West Indies. There is a third plaque which could have been given by John Fuller 'to the memory of the Burrell Family esp. William Burrell Hayley, Rector'. The Burrells and the Hayleys were two Brightling families, which inter-married. William Burrell was a great patron of the arts and was responsible for manuscripts on the history of Sussex, which are now housed in the British Museum. The Rev William Hayley also contributed to the papers. Both were rectors of Brightling. Fuller was an admirer and friend. He had obtained the manuscripts and intended to produce his own history of the county.

William Shield was a prolific composer. Born in County Durham in 1748, he spent his early years playing violin in the North East of England, before coming to London to seek greater recognition. He eventually composed over 60 works and published two books on music. He died in Berner's Street in London at the age of 81. During his life he became a good friend of John Fuller and would have been a frequent guest at musical evenings held at Devonshire Place and Brightling.

There is a slight mystery about his memorial in Brightling Church. Although he has a plaque to his memory in the church, he is actually buried in Westminster Abbey and it is believed this is where it was intended to be displayed. However, it is said the Dean of Westminster objected to the word 'gentleman' being used and refused permission for the memorial to be erected. His reasoning was that after death there are no 'gentlemen'; we are all equal in the eyes of God. Fuller obviously found the Rector of Brightling more tolerant. The words 'buried in Westminster Abbey' were added later.

There is also a memorial erected by Fuller in St Laurence Church, in the nearby village of Catsfield (another Fuller family stronghold). It is to the memory of his uncle — also named John. The sculptor was Joseph Nollekens and it is dated 1810.

Even Brightling Church cannot escape the fanciful tales concerning Fuller. On one occasion when he was dissatisfied with the singing of the choir, the story goes that he provided nine bassoons to accompany them. A variation of this story tells of Fuller visiting a music shop in London and asking which instrument would be suitable to accompany the choir. The proprietor's first suggestion was a trombone. 'Send twelve!' snapped Fuller and walked out of the shop before the startled proprietor could suggest anything else.

His gifts to the church also included the pillars and iron gate and lantern at the entrance to the churchyard.

To the right on leaving the church is a gate leading through to Brightling Park. Fuller is said to have knocked a hole through the wall for his convenience when going to church, an act which greatly annoyed the rector, as Fuller had not first gained his permission to do so. Doubtless the rector was placated with a financial sweetener!

Fuller's uncle — Rose Fuller — during his time at Rose Hill, had altered the direction of the road past the church. Fuller continued this work and had half a mile of new road made from the church towards Brightling Down, and the old road with its beautiful avenue was incorporated into the park. Yet more expense!

And the main reward for all his good deeds for the church? It stands in the corner of the churchyard!

Henry Singleton's portrait of Fuller at the Royal Institution of Great Britain

A Friend to Science

One of the most important aspects of the Industrial Revolution, in the second half of the 18th century, was the flowering of scientific discovery, when the benefits of the marriage of science with industrial endeavour were beginning to be fully realised.

Many scientific societies were formed during this period, initially by like-minded individuals who were drawn together to cultivate their shared interests and ideas for the benefit of others.

By the turn of the century John Fuller had also developed an interest in scientific matters, being especially absorbed by astronomy which fascinated him. He had followed with much interest the refinement of the telescope by Sir William Herschel and had marvelled at the astronomer's discovery of the planet Uranus in 1781. He also expressed keen interest in chemistry and physiology.

At the end of the 18th and the beginning of the 19th centuries, Fuller was to find an outlet, which would enable him to indulge his interests to the full and which, as he grew older, would become a source of great joy as he endeavoured to share his wealth for the benefit of others.

The Royal Institution of Great Britain was founded in 1799 by Benjamin Thompson, for 'diffusing the knowledge and facilitating the general introduction of useful mechanical inventions and improvements, and for teaching by courses of philosophical lectures and experiments the application of science to the common purposes of life'. Premises were taken in Albemarle Street in London and in 1800 the Institution was given a royal charter by King George III.

It must be said that Fuller was not the first of his family to be interested in scientific matters and perhaps he took the lead of his grandfather John and two uncles John and Rose, who had all been members of an earlier-formed organisation, the Royal Society, during the 18th century.

John Fuller was to become a great benefactor to the Royal Institution and a much respected and honoured participant in the running and financing of its work. His name appears on the oldest surviving list of members for 1805, but he was certainly involved before that date and could even have been one of the founder members.

However, his most active period of involvement came after 1828, when he became a life member and there are frequent references to him in the Minutes Book of the Managers and Visitors of the institution. There is also a wealth of information about him in the Institution's library.

His gifts to the Royal Institution were many. By the end of his life he had given over £10,000 to help further its work. His first donation was in 1803 when he subscribed £50 towards the founding of the reference library. He also later furnished the library with a volume of Turner's 'Views of Sussex' and supplied a set of four globe lamps for the Newspaper Room.

On April 21, 1828, Fuller announced an incentive for the progress of chemistry when he offered a gold medal to be given every two years on his birthday, February 20, to 'any person being a Member of the Institution, whom they may consider as having merited the distinction'.

But undoubtedly Fuller's greatest and longest-lasting contribution was the foundation of two professorships. The first was announced in 1833 in the Manager's Minutes as follows: 'Mr Fuller had desired to announce to the Managers that it was his intention provided it met with their wishes, to create a Professorship of Chemistry with a salary of £100 per annum and that he wished Mr Faraday appointed its Professor.' In 1831 Faraday had laid the foundations for the mechanical production of electricity and continued to conduct his experiments through the following years. He was also a frequent lecturer at the Royal Institution.

The second of the Fullerian professorships (of Physiology), was instigated shortly before his death in 1834. The first Professor of Physiology was Dr P M Roget, famous for his 'Thesaurus of English Words and Phrases'. Both professorships became known as the Fullerian Professorships and with each he transferred a sum of over £3000 for their endowment. He lightheartedly referred to the professorships as his 'only two legitimate children'.

He wrote to the Royal Institution telling them that nothing gave him greater satisfaction than to possibly be of service to mankind in general and to his country in particular. Although his health was failing, he

*Pencil sketch of Fuller by
Count d'Orsay, dated 1832*

made every effort to attend lectures. He found peace and tranquillity in the hushed and studious atmosphere of the Royal Institution. Many a time he could be seen at Faraday's lectures, dressed in his old blue coat and white stockings, slumped in a chair, sometimes accidentally nodding off, but always prepared to show his support for the work of the Institution.

During the last two months of his life the ailing Fuller made increasingly determined, almost frantic, efforts to ensure the Royal Institution received more financial help. His correspondence during this time showed he had an almost obsessive desire to share his wealth.

Was there just the slightest hint of guilty conscience to be observed in a letter dated March 24, 1834?: 'I think it is the duty of every man who has lived so long a life as I have done upon the productive labours of society and has no family of his own to provide for, to make society some amends upon that head by supporting an institution which has thrown some of the earliest and most considerable lights on modern philosophy and which promises to discover more.'

To show their gratitude to Fuller the Royal Institution decided to place a bust of him on their premises. In the minutes for March 24 it was resolved to 'consider the best method of obtaining a good bust of Mr Fuller to be placed in some conspicuous place in the house of the Institution'. By means of subscription among the members a sum of £126 was raised towards the cost.

Today it stands proudly among the many other illustrious past members of the Institution. It was made by Sir Francis Chantry and was presented in 1835. The wording below states: 'John Fuller who gave Ten Thousand Pounds for the promotion of science in the Royal Institution'.

His portrait, painted by Henry Singleton, hangs on one of the main stairways and was presented by Fuller to the Institution in 1832.

In the early 19th century, the sciences, along with medicine, relied heavily on the philanthropy of men like Fuller and there seems little doubt he involved himself fully with his benevolence to the Royal Institution. He was a true friend to science.

Michael Faraday, first Fullerian Professor of Chemistry, portrayed today on the reverse of the £20 banknote

FOR THOSE IN PERIL

On July 12, 1832, John Fuller wrote a letter to Professor Michael Faraday at the Royal Institution, enlisting his help with a matter pressing urgently on his mind.

'Sir,

We want something in the practical way to fasten upon an upright buoy which is thrown out from a lifeboat at night in order that a sailor who has been shipwrecked may see it and fasten himself to it until assistance can be given him — if you think of anything that will do and that will show a light — not to be out by the washing of the waves, let me know.

Phosphorus is so difficult to make use of and to keep, I feel it will not do. Anything that will show a good light and is not extinguished will do better.

Sincerely yours

John Fuller'

Fuller's concern for his fellow man had now extended to those in peril on the sea and was prompted by an incident 10 years earlier when, in February 1822, an East Indiaman, *The Thames*, was blown ashore at Eastbourne. A small boat manned by fishermen had put out to assist the crew of 140, when the tiny craft was hit by a giant wave and capsized, resulting in the death of one of its crew.

The event had caused much interest and the sight of *The Thames* lying on the Eastbourne shore proved a great attraction as the curious flocked to the area to view the crippled ship.

Fuller had friends in Eastbourne and had for many years been a frequent visitor to the town, which was then just a small fishing port. On viewing the stranded ship and learning of the loss of life, his awareness of the dangers of the sea were greatly increased. He immediately instructed an Eastbourne boatbuilder, a Mr Simpson, to construct a lifeboat, which he offered to the town. The boat was 25ft long, with a beam of 8ft 6in and rowed by 10 oars. It did not appear to have a name, but was adorned with a rose carved on her bows.

The first sea trial was in October 1822 and she was manned by fishermen and although owned by Fuller, was placed under the care of the Controller of Customs. When Fuller died in 1834 he left the lifeboat 'to the inhabitants of Eastbourne' and she remained in service for a further 30 years. Throughout her life, the boat was launched seven times in earnest, saving 55 lives.

Another act of philanthropy concerning Fuller and the safety of those at sea was his effort to establish a lighthouse on the cliffs above Beachy Head. For many years the stretch of water between Birling Gap and Eastbourne, with its shelf of hard jagged rock, had been a constant source of danger to shipping. In the churchyards of nearby Friston and East Dean are many graves of unknown sailors washed ashore from disasters in the Channel.

Facing page: The crippled Thames stranded on the Eastbourne beach.
Right: The grave of an unknown sailor in Friston churchyard

Fuller arranged to have a lighthouse built on the clifftop in 1828. The structure only served as a temporary measure, but prompted work to start on the erection of the building which occupies the site today — the Belle Tout lighthouse, now a private dwelling. It was completed in 1831 but the lamp was not lit until 1834 and even then did not completely solve the problem as frequent fog and mist obstructed the light. However, it continued to operate until being abandoned in 1900 when the famous lighthouse at the foot of the cliffs came into operation.

In 1923 the Belle Tout was converted to a private dwelling, but abandoned during the last war. It was then badly damaged by misdirected shells from a nearby firing range.

Today it has been restored to good order and is again used as a private residence. In recent years it featured prominently in the television play 'The Lives and Loves of a She Devil'.

Fuller was not the first to appreciate the dangers along this stretch of coast and was perhaps inspired by the exploits of the Reverend Jonathan Darby, Vicar of East Dean in the early 18th century. Greatly troubled by the increasing numbers of unknown burials in his churchyard, he embarked on an incredible scheme to save lives.

Under the point where the Belle Tout now stands, with chisel and axe he hewed out a wide chamber with side recesses for shelter from the wind and connected it to the beach by a sloping tunnel with steps. This man-made cave was reached through a vertical chimney from the cliff top by means of a rope. The Reverend Darby frequently put himself at risk on stormy nights by clambering down to the cave, from where he shone a lantern to warn ships of the dangers. On several occasions he saved the crews of ships battered against the rocks below. The cave became known as 'Darby's Hole', but today nothing remains of this quite remarkable venture. It has long been washed away by the relentless sea.

The Belle Tout in t
late 19th century.
Inset: The shape
see today

Today I Buy a Castle

Situated in the beautiful unspoilt Rother Valley, the moated castle at Bodiam was built in the reign of Richard II by Sir Edward Dalyngrigge, between the years 1385 and 1390 as a precaution against French attack when it was thought necessary to protect a then navigable river.

However, these attacks failed to materialise and only twice did the castle feature in serious conflict; in 1484 when it was captured by Richard III and 1645 during the Civil War when attacked by the parliamentary troops of Sir William Waller.

Nevertheless, despite its lack of history, Bodiam is today regarded as the finest ruined castle in the country. Meticulously maintained by The National Trust, it attracts thousands of visitors each year. It is a beautiful place. However, it has not always been that way.

Bodiam Castle played a part in the life of John Fuller and it would be quite reasonable to state that but for the action of the colourful squire in 1828 there would be no castle to view at all.

For in 1828 Bodiam Castle was nothing more than a decaying, neglected shambles of a building. The damage inflicted during the Civil War in 1645 had been allowed to deteriorate to such a state that the castle was in danger of having to be totally demolished. A firm of Hastings builders stood ready to carry out the task.

However, a last ditch attempt to find a purchaser was made and posters were displayed which declared 'the ancient castle of Bodiham and 25 acres of land' were to be sold by auction under the hammer of Mr George Robins of Covent Garden, London — by direction of a man of rank. The auction would take place 'at the Auction Mart, opposite the Bank of England, on Thursday 18th September 1828, at Twelve o'Clock.'

The man of rank — and owner of the castle at that time — was Baronet Sir Godfrey Webster, of the well-known Sussex family, who were also owners of the nearby Battle Abbey estate.

The Webster family had fallen upon hard times and by 1828 their financial position was dire, mainly due to the extravagant lifestyle and excessive gambling of Sir Godfrey himself. He was a man who entered wholeheartedly into the Georgian obsession with gambling. Many family heirlooms had to be sold to finance his betting mania. On one occasion he wagered an enormous sum on who could pick the longest piece of straw from a haystack and a most wonderful story is told of an amazing race which took place at his London club. He and a companion saw two woodlice crawling along the back of a sofa and they bet on which one would reach the end first. On seeing his chosen insect falling behind, Sir Godfrey pricked it with a pin to hurry it along. Unfortunately for him, it rolled into a ball and played no further part in the contest. Sir Godfrey lost a small fortune!

Left: Bodiam Castle in 1831. Below: The medal struck by Fuller to commemorate his acquisition of Bodiam Castle and to aid Hastings' first hospital for the poor.

Bodiam Castle had been in the family since the early 18th century and through their years of ownership had deteriorated to a sad state. They were unable to raise the finances needed to maintain the building.

Sir Godfrey had held the manor of Bodiam since 1800 and had previously contemplated selling it in 1815. A printed prospectus of the impending sale was drawn up in that year, but there was no conclusion to the affair. By 1828 financial necessity prevailed. This time a sale was imperative.

While discussing the Webster family, it would appear their administration and maintenance of both Bodiam Castle and Battle Abbey left much to be desired. Whether caused by their lack of funds or of a lack of any sense of history, the treatment of both places was far from sympathetic. Due to the actions of earlier generations of the family, especially at Battle Abbey (surely one of the most historic sites in the world), much of our heritage was lost.

Pointers to the family's attitude to ancient monuments can be found in the early 18th century, when the then owner of Battle Abbey, Sir Whistler Webster demolished important 16th century buildings on the estate and in the early 19th century the roof of the dormitory block of the abbey was ripped off and the building used for stabling horses. Their respect for historic buildings seemed rather callous to say the least.

Such was the sorry condition of the abbey estate in 1742 that the architect Sir Horace Walpole was prompted to note that 'the grounds, and what has been the park, lie in a vile condition'. It would appear that Bodiam Castle had declined to the same level in 1828. Thankfully, this time there was a saviour.

Whether John Fuller's purchase of Bodiam Castle was fired by high ideals can only be guessed at, but it is very probable that his philanthropic spirit did come to the fore to save the castle for his beloved country and county of Sussex. Or perhaps he just felt it suited his colourful character to own a castle. His friends at his London club would have been most impressed!

Whatever the reasons, 3000 guineas (as stated in the draft agreement dated November 18, 1828) was not a large sum for John Fuller to pay and the sale of the castle and 24 acres, 3 roods, 8 perches was duly completed by his solicitors, Barton and Bellingham of Battle, on February 14, 1829.

A Sussex newspaper at the time described the new owner as the 'eccentric Squire of Brightling', and Fuller soon set about making essential repairs to the castle. In 1831 a new set of folding oak gates were erected at the main entrance door and restoration was completed on the southern or Postern Tower.

A year earlier Fuller had issued an attractive coin to celebrate his ownership of Bodiam Castle. The coin also commemorated another of his acts of philanthropy. On the front was an illustration of the castle and on the reverse a declaration of his support for Hastings' first infirmary for the poor.

On December 9, 1829, a meeting had been convened in the Town Hall at Hastings to consider the establishment of a dispensary for the relief of the sick poor in that town and its adjacent parishes. It was agreed that the scheme would be supported by subscriptions from 'the nobility, gentry and inhabitants of the town and its neighbourhood and other voluntary aids'. The dispensary was eventually established in High

IN SUSSEX.

Particulars and Conditions of Sale
OF THE FOLLOWING VERY VALUABLE
FREEHOLD PROPERTY,
VIZ.
THE ANCIENT
CASTLE OF BODIHAM,
AND ABOUT
25 ACRES OF LAND;
ALSO
The MANOR of BODIHAM,
THE PERPETUAL ADVOWSON,
RIGHT OF PRESENTATION, AND PATRONAGE OF
THE VICARAGE OF HOOE,
AND VICARIAL TITHES OVER
2,500 ACRES.
THE MANOR OF BARNHORNE,
AND
BARNHORNE FARM, NEAR HASTINGS,
CONTAINING ABOUT
300 ACRES
Of excellent LAND, in a Ring Fence.
A FARM OF FORTY ACRES,
Called KITCHINGHAMS, situate at
HOOE AND BEXHILL;
AND
THE ROYAL OAK PUBLIC HOUSE;
Which will be Sold by Auction
BY
Mr. GEO⁴· ROBINS

At the Auction Mart, opposite the Bank of England,
On THURSDAY, 18th SEPTEMBER, 1828, at Twelve o'Clock,
In EIGHT LOTS, by Direction of a MAN of RANK.

Particulars may be had Fourteen Days prior to the Sale, at the principal Inns at Eastbourne, Hastings, Battle, Lewes, and Brighton; of Messrs. CAPRON, ROWLEY, and WELD, Saville Place, New Burlington Street; the Auction Mart; and at Mr. GEORGE ROBINS's Offices, Covent Garden, London.

James Whiting, Beaufort House.

Street and Fuller played his full part in helping to finance the project. His nephew, Augustus Elliot Fuller, continued the good work after Fuller's death in 1834.

Bodiam Castle stayed in the Fuller family until 1864, when it was sold to Mr George Cubitt, MP (later Lord Ashcombe), for £5000. In 1919, the authoress and poet, Vita Sackville West and her husband Harold Nicolson (famous for their gardens at Sissinghurst Castle), considered buying Bodiam and converting the surviving towers into a home, but it was eventually bought that year by Lord Curzon, the Marquis of Kedleston, KG, who continued the improvement work and set about returning the castle to its former glory. He eventually bequeathed it to The National Trust in 1925.

Lord Curzon had devoted his life to restoring the building to what we see today and happily the castle had fallen into the hands of a caring owner.

But for our story, it is pleasant to reflect that if it had not been for John Fuller's intervention in 1828 there would have been little to restore and Bodiam Castle would have been just a few crumbling stones.

Bodiam Castle today

THE PATHS OF GLORY...

On March 26, 1834, the Royal Institution of Great Britain received its last correspondence from John Fuller. He knew he was dying and it had been a considerable time since he had last been able to attend its meetings.

In the letter he thanked the Institution for 'the very handsome notice' they had taken of his endeavours and he forwarded his gratitude to the members who had subscribed towards the cost of the marble bust.

John Fuller died in the afternoon of Friday, April 11 at his home in Devonshire Place. *The Times* newspaper reported on April 14: 'Mr Faraday, at the conclusion of his lecture at the Royal Institution on Friday night, received information, which he immediately communicated to his auditors, of the death of this celebrated and venerable gentleman who, for several days past, has been in an almost hopeless state.' The report wrongly stated that 'His parliamentary career was rendered memorable by an insult to the Speaker, for which he was committed to the Tower,' but concluded with a most accurate reflection: 'He was a gentleman much esteemed for his social qualities.'

The funeral was arranged for the following Friday and as a mark of respect, the Royal Institution voted to close its doors during the whole day. It was also noted in the Manager's Minutes that the porters, library assistants and housemaids of the Institution be provided with suitable mourning clothes.

In many obituaries Fuller was glowingly acclaimed for his public spirited generosity to the Royal Institution. One described him as a 'zealous and warm patron'. In the Annual Reports of the Royal Institution for the years 1834 and 1835 his generosity and dedication were recorded with deep gratitude and much sadness at his demise.

In keeping with a man of his stature, a medallion was struck after his

JACK FULLER.
A DEPARTED FRIEND TO SCIENCE.

death for distribution to mourners. On one side was his portrait and on the other his age and date of death. An engraving was also issued in which he was described as 'A Departed Friend to Science'. Of that there is no doubt.

John Fuller's will was dated November 5, 1823, but by the time of his death 17 codicils, mostly written on half sheets of paper, had been added — an indication of the last frantic efforts the dying Fuller had made to make sure everyone benefited.

The bulk of his fortune and Sussex estates including Rose Hill, along with his Jamaican interests, were left to his nephew Augustus Elliot Fuller, and the London estates to another nephew, Sir Peregrine Palmer Acland, Bart.

The sum of £1000 was bequeathed to 'Sophia Foley, otherwise Williams, spinster, who now resides with me'. The lady was presumably his housekeeper. Whatever her role in his life, she was obviously a great favourite, for Fuller also directed that 'my executors hereinafter named to pay her the same within three calendar months next after my death'. The painter of his portrait and one of the witnesses of his will, Henry Singleton, was left £100, as was Fuller's servant Thomas. Among many other bequests were those to his solicitors, Messrs Barton and Bellingham of Battle and the composer, William Shield.

Fuller left his books, furniture, telescopes and instruments to the person who would come into possession of Rose Hill and a friend Major Forbes of Heathfield, received 20 guineas to purchase a ring 'on account of their friendship'.

An indication of the spread of the Fuller family across the British Isles can be seen in codicil 2, in which Fuller appoints as an additional executor, Owen John Augustus Fuller Meyrick of Bodorgan in the Island of Anglesey, North Wales.

In codicil 12, dated February 8, 1834, Fuller's enlightened views on medical matters can clearly be seen when he stated: 'I do also desire my body to be opened if it is thought necessary to know the cause of my death.'

The reluctance of the church to sanction post-mortem examinations had been a stumbling block to medical progress for many years and had merely encouraged the snatching of freshly-buried bodies from graves for illegal research. However, throughout the 18th century, medical science had slowly emerged from the dark ages of superstition and by the time of Fuller's death, a more flexible attitude was beginning to prevail.

Whether the option of a post-mortem was acted upon is not known,

The coin struck to commemorate Fuller's death

nor the exact reasons (apart from old age) for his death. Perhaps his massive frame had at last proved too stern a task for an ageing heart, or as he knew he was dying for several months previous, it could have been some form of tumour which eventually killed him.

And so John Fuller took his last journey to Brightling. *The Gentleman's Magazine* recorded that his funeral cortège was 'attended out of London by twenty-four private carriages'. He was interred, according to his wishes, in the 25ft high pyramid at Brightling, which had been ready and waiting for him for 24 years in the churchyard adjacent to his home. One harrowing thought is that during those years he would have been able to see the top of his grave-to-be over the dividing wall.

On the wall of the interior of the tomb is the 9th verse of Thomas Gray's 'Elegy in a Country Churchyard', which seems to sum up the disillusionment he was feeling at the time the pyramid was built:

'The boast of heraldry, the pomp of pow'r
And all that beauty, all that wealth e'er gave
Await alike th' inevitable hour
The paths of glory lead but to the grave.'

Fuller was not the first (or the last) to be buried in a pyramid in this country. Indeed it may have been a family trait! At Nether Wallop Church in Hampshire one can see the pyramid grave of Francis Douce, a distant relative of Fuller, whose tomb was also erected as the result of a deal made with the church authorities. Douce died in 1760 and in his will he left money to the parish on condition that his pyramid was well maintained after his death. Did Francis Douce's actions inspire Fuller to build his own mausoleum?

Another pyramid builder was Douce's cousin, Paulet St John, but in this case it did not serve as his tomb. Around 1733 he built a pyramid on top of Farley Mount in Hampshire, in memory of his horse.

There is also another fine pyramid tomb at Blickling Hall in Norfolk, now administered by The National Trust. It is the last resting place of the second Earl of Buckingham and his two wives. It stands 45 feet high and was built in 1794. A later more modest five feet high pyramid can be found at Attleborough churchyard, the grave of Norfolk solicitor, 'Lawyer' Brooke, who died in 1929 and had left precise instructions as to the measurements and quality of limestone to be used for his last resting place.

Owing to the unusual nature of Fuller's grave, several outrageous stories have been handed down through the years. One states that he left instructions to be interred sitting at an iron table, a full meal before him, a bottle of claret at arm's length, dressed for dinner and wearing a top hat. The floor was said to be strewn with broken glass in order to

Inspiration for Mr Fuller? The tomb of Francis Douce at Nether Wallop, Hampshire

keep the Devil out until he was ready to enter his tomb and stay there forever.

It is a lovely tale and typical of those told about John Fuller; stories dreamed up by the locals, either through ignorance or merely to impress the gullible visitor. It would be fascinating if the tale of unusual burial were true, but sadly there were no such instructions in Fuller's will. It plainly stated: 'I direct that my body shall be interred under the pavement in the mausoleum in the churchyard at Brightling aforesaid which is made over to me by the Bishops faculty.'

Fuller's mausoleum originally had large wooden doors at the entrance which, during the 1920s, were replaced by bricks when the

*No simple gravestone for Mr Fuller.
For the last 24 years of his life Fuller could see
his extravagant grave-to-be from his adjoining
estate*

timber began to rot. It was around this time that the story of unconventional burial seems to have been nurtured for the benefit of curious visitors. Brightling was a popular venue for hundreds of charabanc outings from the seaside resorts during the summer months and drivers would beguile their passengers with this and other extravagant tales of John Fuller.

In 1982, it was decided to remove the brickwork blocking the entrance to the tomb and again the story became very 'hot' news. The local newspapers fired the imagination of readers with headlines such as: 'Will Jack Fuller be found sitting at a table?' and 'Will the mystery be solved?'.

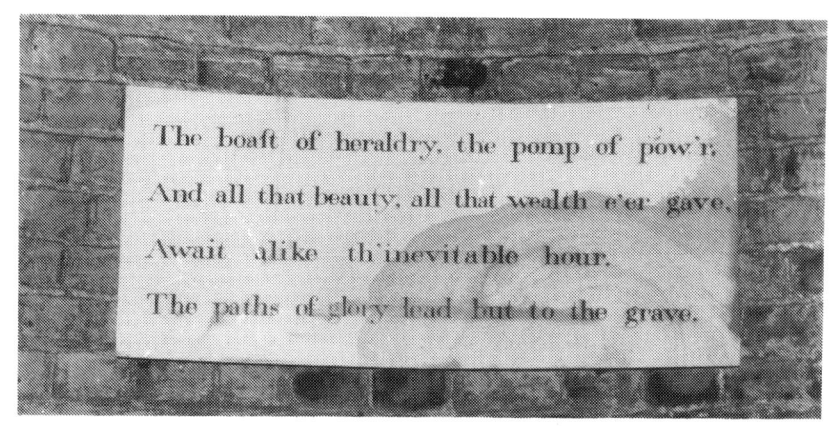

The ninth verse of Gray's 'Elegy in a Country Churchyard,' on the interior wall of the pyramid

Of course, there was no mystery to be solved. Needless to say, Fuller is buried beneath the floor in the conventional manner. The entrance was later covered by an iron grille and today, although most of the bricks have been replaced, one can still look into the tomb where Gray's verse can be seen on the facing wall.

During 1987 cracks began to appear at the base of the pyramid and it was feared the structure could be slipping. A fund was set up, the foundations checked and the necessary remedial work was successfully carried out.

Fuller was not alone when it came to rumours of unusual burial. Among the popular crazes in late Georgian and Victorian times was to be buried head first in the ground. The story goes that a Major Labellière was so interred at Box Hill in Surrey, so that when Judgment Day came and the world turned upside down, he would be on his feet, ready to greet his maker. Another rather daft story is centred around the spectacular 170 feet high May's Folly at Hadlow in Kent. Among the various stories concerning the tower's origins is one that says its builder, Walter Barton May, feared that his estate would pass from the hands of his family if he were not buried above ground.

And as for the tale about keeping the Devil from Fuller's pyramid; stories of devils in tombs were frequent in Sussex when smuggling was in its heyday, with graveyards being used as hiding places for contraband. A good example was at nearby Northiam, where 18th century smugglers would store their ill-gotten gains among the coffins

Above: The interior of the pyramid. Left: The domed ceiling

in the Frewen mausoleum in the churchyard. The practice continued until the entrance was bricked up in 1786.

A Devil story was usually enough to keep the curious away. Could Mr Fuller have been involved in smuggling? Most people were in those days — even clergymen were not unknown to succumb to the temptation!

Although Fuller had earlier spoke out strongly against the illicit trade in the House of Commons in 1805, during his Parliamentary days, perhaps he later had a change of heart!

Another popular story connected with tombs and indeed, any building of unusual design, is the hermit story, and this is mentioned in connection with the pyramid. It is said that Fuller twice advertised for a hermit to occupy the pyramid while he was still alive. The person was not allowed to shave, cut his hair, or wash and have no contact with other folk. He had to stay there for one year and if the poor unfortunate survived the year Fuller would have made him a gentleman for life.

However, it is highly improbable the tale is true in the case of the pyramid, because he would not have gained permission as the structure was in the churchyard. To erect such a massive building was surely outrageous enough!

Nevertheless, if the hermit story is not applicable to the pyramid, there is certainly an element of truth in other instances. Although the treatment of hermits was not as severe or cruel as described above, it is a known fact that certain rich landowners did encourage such people to occupy designated areas of their estates, to provide a form of entertainment and amusement for themselves and visitors.

As you have read, according to the entry in the Burials and Baptism Register, Fuller made a deal with the vicar over the tomb. He got his tomb and the church got a new wall, which prevented earth slipping

No 2, The Street, Brightling, formerly The Green Man pub

down into the road after heavy rain. The church also received the gift of two substantial stone pillars and an iron gate.

Even this has been embellished over the years and it is said that Fuller could only gain permission for the tomb if he moved the public house 'The Green Man', which he owned, from the village centre, to stop villagers drinking instead of attending church on Sundays.

It is true there was a pub called 'The Green Man' opposite the church and it is possible the vicar *did* ask if the pub could be moved, but it is unlikely there is any connection with the building of the pyramid. The only pub throughout the years since has been 'The Fuller's Arms', a converted barn, of which Fuller was again the owner, situated ½ mile from the village. It retained this name until recent years, when it was renamed 'Jack Fullers' and now functions solely as a restaurant.

Even after dismissing the fanciful tales and cutting through the myths, Fuller's pyramid still has a certain magical fascination about it. Just what thoughts were going through his mind when he decided to have it erected? Did he really think his life was coming to an end in 1811? Was this massive structure the result of a fit of post-Parliamentary depression? Did he have fantasies of ancient Egypt? Was it some form of Masonic ritual? — or was he just laughing at death?

Although a man of his position could easily have gained permission to be buried on his own land, it would appear he wished to be buried with his people in the churchyard of a place he loved dearly, in a manner which reflected his larger-than-life persona. No simple gravestone would have done for John Fuller!

Miss Bessie Russell, now in her late eighties and having lived most of her life in Brightling, provides us with a modern day link to Fuller's times. She relates that her great great grandmother, Sophia, actually watched Fuller's funeral procession wend its way through the village to the churchyard on that day in 1834. Sophia lived to the grand old age of 92 and her recollections have been passed down through the years.

Bessie also provided an added theory to the story of his unconventional burial. According to the Russell family grapevine, when Fuller's coffin was first placed inside the pyramid it was laid between two iron chairs. It remained in this position for several days and it was only buried beneath the floor when it was deemed necessary to sort out Fuller's affairs. According to law that could not be done until his body was six feet under! Could that be how the fanciful story of burial aboveground took shape? Were the top hat, table and chicken meal an embellishment to add flavour to the tale? Who knows? After all, everyone loves a good yarn!

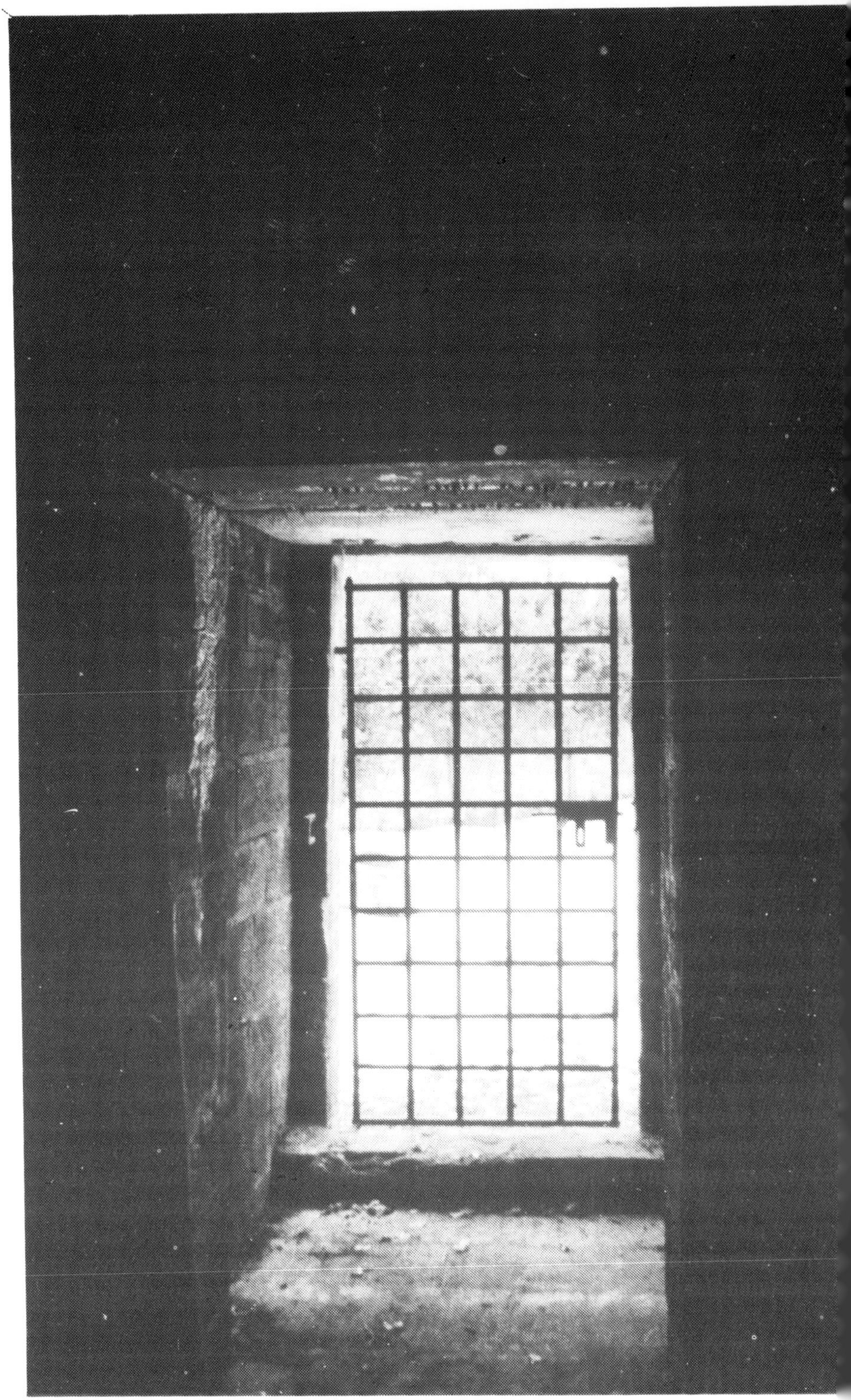

LEGACY: THE BUILDINGS AND FOLLIES

For all John Fuller's attempts throughout his eventful life to perpetuate his name, it is the odd collection of buildings littered around his estate which provide the stimulus to investigate him further. They are his legacy which makes people curious. Almost certainly that was his intention.

His buildings mark the end of one chapter of his life and the start of another; they divide the ambitious, aggressive character of his early days from the more gentle caring side he showed in the latter years. It can be surmised the last 24 years of his life gave him vastly more pleasure than those that passed before.

It seems quite wrong to label some of his structures as follies at all as they had a definite purpose. His observatory, for instance, was built to view the stars. What else would an observatory be used for! Even his tomb, as weird and as wonderful as it is, had its obvious purpose.

The last section of this book will examine Fuller's buildings, the extravagant stories told about them and attempt to explain the true reason for their construction. As there is very little documentation, there has to be much supposition.

Many theories have been put forward, from the sublime to the ridiculous. Some believe the follies stand on ley lines or that Fuller's buildings were part of a nationwide signalling system or that the Egyptian imagery portrayed by the pyramid and obelisk reflect his involvement in freemasonry. Many of the more extravagant tales are the result of inventive minds — and ignorance.

The first Fullerian venture into architectural creation took place in 1803 in the shape of a small semi-circular summerhouse situated in the woods to the west side of Brightling Park. The front of the summer-

house is in the form of an ornamental arch and is made from Coadestone, an artificial stone, very popular between 1760 and 1820
The simple summerhouse was the first. There were far more spectacular attempts to follow.

The first of Jack Fuller's buildings, the Coadestone summerhouse. Erected in 1803, it had in recent years fallen into disrepair. In 1992 English Heritage provided the funds for its complete restoration.

The Rotunda Temple

In the final paragraph of Repton's report on Rose Hill, he mentions the placing of a structure on the hillock facing the house. The Rotunda Temple is almost certainly the result.

This pleasant little garden temple is probably the only idea in Humphry Repton's suggestions which appealed to John Fuller and it is believed he involved Robert Smirke in its design.

Situated in the middle of Brightling Park on top of a little slope, the circular domed building follows the Grecian style. It is 25ft high and has steps leading up to a door which faces the mansion. On either side of the door is a window and the structure stands on a base three to four feet high with pillars surrounding a circular room. A section of the base is hollow and was probably used to store food and wine to be consumed when visits were made to the Temple on hot summer days.

It is difficult to date the erection of the Temple but it is believed to have been built around 1810, as this date corresponds with Smirke's visits to Rose Hill. A further pointer can be gleaned from the fact that the structure is clearly shown in Turner's scenic view of the Rose Hill estate, which was painted during the latter half of that year.

From a distance, the Temple is simply a pleasant eyecatcher, very common in landscaped gardens of the period. However, as it was situated on John Fuller's land and not readily accessible, curious villagers would invent their own reasons for its construction and for such a simple, inoffensive building, the Temple has attracted more than its fair share of strange tales through the years. One local story states that it was used for gambling sessions. It is said that Fuller would entertain his friends at Rose Hill and after dinner, escort them to the Temple, where they would play cards for extremely high stakes.

Another suggestion is that Fuller entertained his lady friends there; ladies of ill-repute and the building was the scene of many a wild orgy.

It all sounds quite enthralling, but on closer inspection of the Temple, one finds the interior extremely cramped; the members of a card school would have been most uncomfortable and there certainly would not

have been enough room (considering Fuller's size) to indulge in frenzied orgies! Although we have established that Fuller did enjoy the company of ladies, the thought of his massive frame cavorting after the 'ladies of the night' around the Temple, does seem a little amusing — and most unlikely!

Another wild, but equally entertaining, tale states that a tunnel linked the structure to the mansion — a distance of over half a mile. Mrs Grissell, the former owner of Brightling Park, says that no evidence of such a tunnel was ever found during demolition work carried out during the 1950s, on the side of the house facing the Temple. Had it existed it would certainly have been exposed.

Perhaps with these stories of tunnels, gambling and orgies, Fuller was being compared to an earlier, more famous 18th century exponent of the weird and unusual — Sir Francis Dashwood of West Wycombe. Sir Francis, like Fuller, was a Member of Parliament and became one of the most outrageous Chancellors of the Exchequer of all time. During his time in Parliament he was an acquaintance of Rose Fuller.

As well as erecting strange structures around his estate (including a rotunda Temple) and outwardly presenting an image of respectability, Dashwood was the founder of The Knights of St Francis of Wycombe, later to become the notorious Hell-Fire Club, whose members consisted of some of the most eminent men of the time. The club would hold its meetings in the caves which ran under Dashwood's estate, where lavish parties, heavy drinking and whoring took place at regular intervals.

Even the local church, which stood within view of his mansion, could not escape his eccentricity. Dashwood erected a giant golden globe above the bell-chamber of the 14th century church tower (it is still there), big enough to accommodate up to ten people, where it is said the irreverent members of the Hell-Fire Club would hold card parties.

Was Fuller, in his own way, trying to ape Sir Francis? Along with many others, he would have been well versed with the stories and may have even visited West Wycombe to see for himself. Perhaps his Temple at Brightling was an attempt to emulate the antics of Sir Francis. More likely, the idea was sown by local people who wanted to believe their colourful squire was up to something weird. We'll never know for sure!

It was also implied that Fuller's Temple could have been used as a storage room for smuggled wares, or even a hide-out for smugglers. As previously stated, Fuller had publicly voiced his disapproval of smuggling in 1805, but perhaps by 1810 he had adopted the attitude: 'If you can't beat them, join them'!

The tales connected to the Temple are typical of those surrounding all of Fuller's buildings. They have been embellished through the years and Fuller would no doubt be delighted to know people are still talking — and puzzling — about him today.

The Rotunda Temple is on private land and can only be viewed from a considerable distance. One of the best vantage points is on the road from Netherfield to Woods Corner. A closer and more romantic view is from Brightling Park cricket ground, where the local side play regular matches throughout the summer. It is an idyllic setting and there can surely be no finer (or rarer) backdrop to an English cricket match than a Georgian Grecian Temple!

The Obelisk

For a Georgian gentleman to adorn his grounds with an eyecatching obelisk, was considered most appropriate. The erection of such a structure on a country estate, whether purely for decoration or to celebrate an event or deed, was deemed an extremely fashionable thing to do. Many hundreds, of all sizes, were erected across the British Isles in those times.

The Brightling obelisk, more popularly known as the Brightling Needle, stands to the north-west of Brightling Park. It is 65 feet high and stands on the site of a former beacon at the second highest point of Sussex, 646 feet above sea level and is regularly used as a surveyor's point. It is built of stone blocks and is situated on private land in a field approximately 200 yards from the road. The reasons for its erection are not recorded. Again John Fuller keeps us guessing!

One theory is that it may have been designed by Robert Smirke to celebrate Wellington's victory over Napoleon in 1815. Fuller was a great admirer of the Iron Duke (the inscribed bells in the church tower bear witness to this) and it is possible he could have commissioned Smirke to draw the plans. The architect was a regular visitor to Rose Hill and was at this time involved in the design of many such obelisk memorials to Wellington (not all came to fruition), the most famous being at Phoenix Park in Dublin. This structure does bear a marked resemblance to the construction at Brightling. But which came first? Perhaps the Brightling Needle was the prototype of the Dublin monument and Smirke was given the opportunity by John Fuller to try out his design in a less conspicuous place.

Another possibility is that the obelisk was to commemorate Nelson (another of Fuller's heroes) in or after 1805. This would mean Smirke was not the designer as his first visit to Rose Hill was in 1810. Fuller was always ready to demonstrate his patriotism. On his estate at Brightling he was in possession of several small cannons — probably relics of his volunteer militia days — and after Nelson's victory at Trafalgar, he considered that a cannon salute would be a most appropriate way to mark the great naval commander's triumph. Sadly it ended in disaster, when one of the cannons exploded, killing his butler. The bizarre event is described in *The Observer* newspaper of November 24, 1805.

If the structure was intended as a memorial, it is surprising that there is no inscription to mark the fact. If the Georgians lacked anything, it was certainly not words! This strange omission leads to the assumption that the most probable reason for its construction was purely as an amusement; a decoration for the estate and most importantly, to provide work for the villagers during the years of severe unemployment. This was almost certainly the thinking behind many of Fuller's building projects.

Over the years the Needle fell into disrepair, but in 1985, funds were made available for its renovation, and a sum of £22,000 was spent on strengthening and stabilising the structure. The repair work was timely. The Needle would almost certainly have succumbed to the hurricane force winds of 1987. Experts now say it is good for another 100 years!

At the summit of the Needle are two interesting inscriptions scratched into the cement. The first reads: 'R Croft, 1899' and the second: 'Charles Croft, July 29 1889, aged 16 years', marks left by members of the local family building firm of that name, during earlier repair work.

The Observatory

Fuller's increasing interest in the sciences in the early 19th century also caused him some frustration. His particular fascination was astronomy, but he lacked the facilities to pursue his interest. Fuller soon found a solution. He built his own Observatory!

The result is the odd-shaped tiered building surmounted by an oriental silver dome, which stands high on the Brightling skyline on the road to Burwash.

Fuller spared no expense on the building. It was well furnished with the most sophisticated equipment of the time and once contained a camera-obscura. The inspiration for the Observatory is believed to have come from his friend, the famous astronomer, Sir William Herschel (1738-1822), who discovered the planet Uranus. It appears Fuller either intended to temporarily reside in the building or to have a resident astronomer present on site, as on the plans for the building there is provision for living quarters.

It is the only building of which there is definite evidence of Sir Robert Smirke's involvement. He designed it in 1810 and the structure was completed in 1818. The original plans are housed at the Royal Institute of Architects in London.

After Fuller's death, according to records in the library of The Royal Institution of Great Britain, the Observatory was run by a committee and later became a museum. How long this continued is not known as there is a substantial gap in the building's history and it would appear it fell into a neglected state.

In 1952 it was purchased by a local antiques dealer, who sunk a well and installed plumbing, but he did not live in it. The property changed hands several times after and was eventually used as a residence, but it was not until the 1960s that the Observatory possessed more modern amenities, with the addition of central heating and other modern comforts, when it was purchased for the sum of £5,500 by a retired naval officer, Commander Hugh Malleson and his wife.

Commander Malleson, a keen amateur astronomer, set about the task of restoring the building to its original use. He replaced the wooden, lead-covered dome with an aluminium substitute, a section of which could be slid open. He installed electricity to the dome to enable it to be revolved and from this high vantage point, with an 8½ inch diameter reflector telescope, he could pursue his favourite hobby.

Robert Smirke's plan for the Observatory

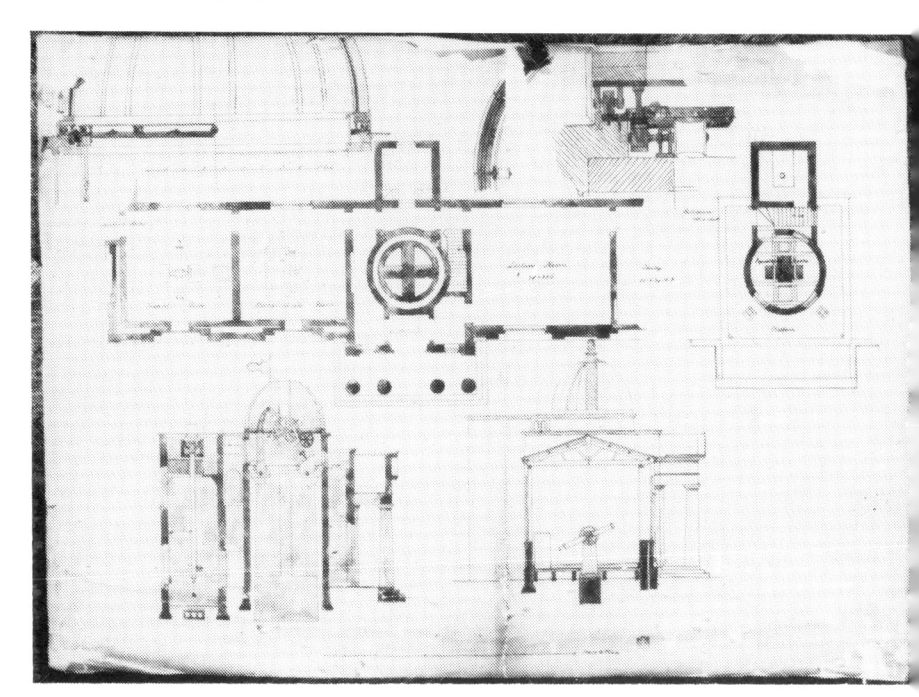

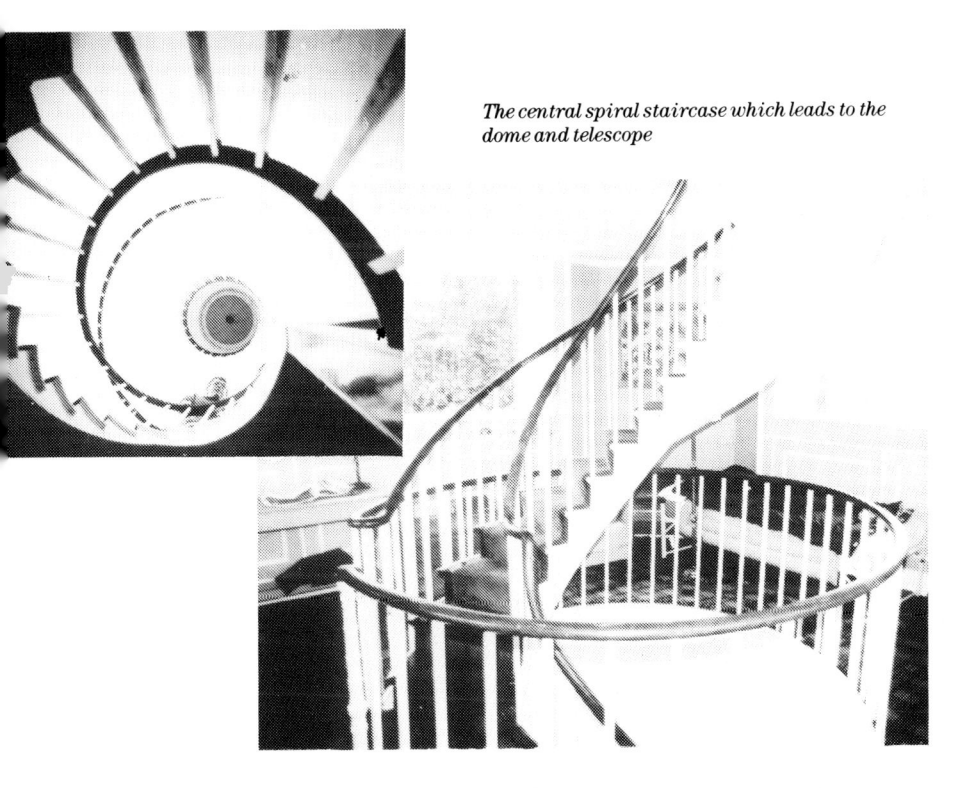

The central spiral staircase which leads to the dome and telescope

Above the dome he installed a wind direction indicator and an anemometer for measuring its force. A wind speed exceeding 20 miles per hour meant it was too dangerous to open the dome.

The equipment is still in place today and the present owner continues to use the Observatory for its intended purpose. He, too, is a dedicated stargazer!

The padlock-shaped building has a most attractive interior with a central spiral staircase leading to a square platform-floor, affording magnificent views across the surrounding countryside, with most of Fuller's buildings being able to be seen to maximum effect.

From this level the staircase continues up to a trap door which opens into the dome.

The Observatory is a quite remarkable building. It has a bright and cheerful ambience and seems to reflect the jolly side of John Fuller.

Even though the Observatory had a very definite purpose, it still has not escaped the customary folly-story being attached to it. It is told that the servants, using the telescope no less, looked out for signs of John Fuller's coach returning from London in order to put the kettle on and put everything in a state of welcome.

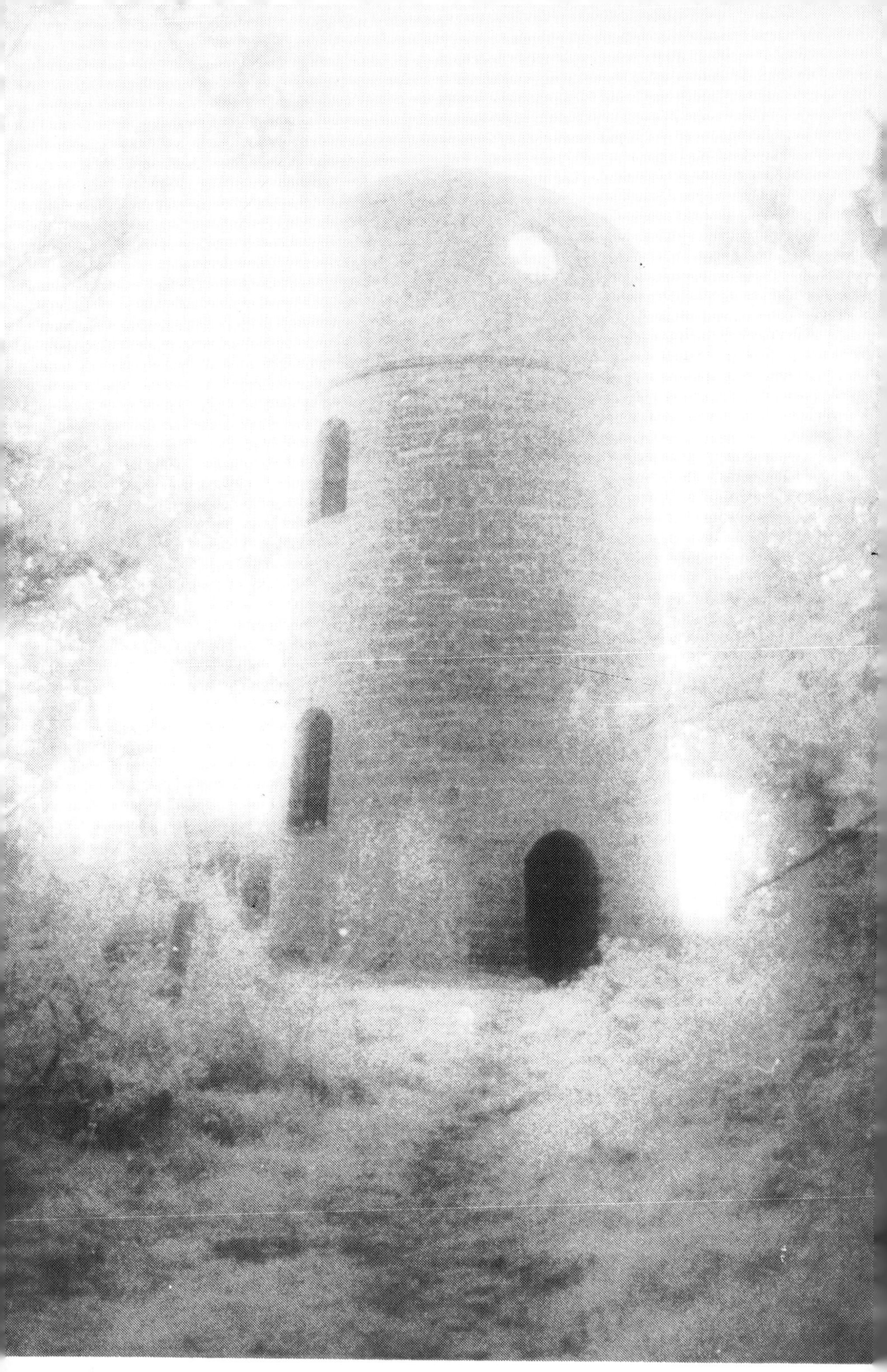

The Tower

The Brightling tower is situated a little over a quarter-of-a-mile southeast of Brightling Park, off the Brightling-Darwell Hole road. It stands at the top of a hill and can be reached by a footpath.

It is a 35 feet high stone-built circular building, 12 feet in diameter, with a Gothic entrance, four windows and a castellated top. Originally there were two floors.

The tower provides one of Fuller's greatest puzzles. The date it was built and the reasons for its construction can only be guessed, but the most popular and logical theory is that it was connected with Fuller's purchase of Bodiam Castle in 1828. It is suggested that it played a part in some form of signalling system between Brightling and Bodiam, some six miles distant. The castle can be seen from the top of the tower and may be Fuller would keep a watchful eye on the progress of the repairs being carried out. Similarly, the workmen, by using flags or mirrors, could signal for replenishment of materials.

The tower is sometimes referred to as the Hermit's Tower and has the same story attached to it as the pyramid; that some poor unfortunate would be compelled to inhabit it for a year, without any form of comfort and be rewarded by the master at the end of his year of denial.

Perhaps, along with the estate wall and other buildings, the tower was erected simply to provide much-needed employment and, of course, to put another feather in John Fuller's cap in his efforts to compete with his neighbours. If anyone else had a tower, why shouldn't Mr Fuller!

Several were completed in Sussex in Georgian times with the flimsiest of excuses for their erection. These were eccentric, never-to-be-repeated, days! Among the best examples are the Toat Monument at Pulborough, which marks the spot where Samuel Drinkald fell from his horse; the Gibraltar Tower at Heathfield, built to commemorate the deeds of General Elliott during the siege of Gibraltar; the Saxonbury Tower at Eridge, erected purely for the views it commands; and the five-storey Racton Tower in West Sussex which enabled Lord Halifax to watch shipping in Chichester Harbour. There is also a squat tower at West Firle on the South Downs which, like the Brightling tower, is said to have been used for signalling purposes.

Fuller's tower at Brightling was, until 1987, enclosed in the middle of a copse and was barely noticeable in the summer months when the trees were in full foliage. However, many of the trees were blown over by the hurricane winds of 1987 and the tower itself also suffered damage from the falling timber. Thankfully, it has since been repaired.

Whatever the reasons for its erection, today it is an eerie mysterious building, which provokes a feeling of unease; that one shouldn't really be there at all! It is hard to explain. The feeling was even more intense when the structure was surrounded by trees.

Originally the tower had a wooden staircase, but this was destroyed by fire during the 1920s. Bessie Russell again helps to paint a clearer picture. She was about 12 years old at the time when, one day around lunchtime, she and the villagers noticed a thick pall of smoke rising from the tower. Bessie has a fairly good idea who was responsible, but she names no names. Suffice to say, boys will be boys and matches have always held a fascination for the young!

In more recent years the British Gypsum Company, in conjunction with the Sussex Historic Gardens Restoration Society, has been involved with the renovation of the structure and an iron staircase has been installed.

The views from the tower are most spectacular and well worth the effort of the climb to the top. A novel way of pinpointing the position of Bodiam, without the aid of binoculars, is to watch out for the hot air balloons which rise from the castle grounds when weather conditions are favourable.

Victim of the storm winds of 1987

The Sugar Loaf

The term Sugar Loaf derives from bygone days when sugar was sold in a solid cone-shaped mass and because of its shape this fascinating building has taken the same name. It stands 35 feet high on a circular base 15 feet in diameter and is situated in the south-west side of Brightling Park in a meadow off the Battle-Heathfield road near the hamlet of Woods Corner. There is an entrance porch and only one of its several windows remains unblocked. The structure can be viewed at close quarters by using the public footpath which runs alongside.

John Fuller's Sugar Loaf is a delight! It represents the epitome of folly building. Not only is it a stunning eyecatcher, it has a wickedly devious — but quite feasible — story attached to it.

It is said that Fuller made a wager that he could see, from his house, the spire of St Giles Church in the neighbouring village of Dallington to the south. On discovering he could not, due to the intervening hill between the two places, he swiftly had the Sugar Loaf erected to win the bet.

Its a lovely story and could well be true! It cannot be denied that there is a remarkable similarity between the top of Dallington Church and the Sugar Loaf and furthermore the structure has been described as 'nothing more than stones held together by mud', which suggests it was erected in a great rush.

There are two versions of how and where the wager was made. One says that it was while Fuller was entertaining one evening at Rose Hill that the subject was lightheartedly raised over dinner. As it was dark there was no way of proving the fact one way or another and it was not until the following morning that Fuller, being first to rise, discovered the error of his claim and in panic ordered the building to be quickly erected before his guests rose for breakfast. A tall order!

The second story suggests that he was in his London club when he made his extravagant claim. Although there is no documented evidence of Fuller belonging to a gentlemen's club in London (not all have members' lists dating back that far), it is a pretty fair assumption to

The Sugar Loaf: The epitome of folly building

believe a man of his stature would have belonged to one of the three major establishments founded in Georgian times — Whites, Brooks's or Boodles. Boodles of St James's Street would appear to be the most likely. It was established in 1762 in Pall Mall and later moved to its present elegant rooms in 1783. Members were mostly country gentlemen, but also included some famous men of the time, among them Beau Brummell and Fuller's great favourite, the Duke of Wellington. Boodles had a reputation for gambling and good food. As we know, one of these certainly appealed to Fuller. Why not the other?

Gambling, eating, drinking — and even duelling — were the pastimes of English gentlemen in Georgian times. Whole estates were sometimes lost around the gaming table and no matter how frivolous the wager, there was always a taker.

So, this is how the chain of events may have progressed. Fuller, full of port, probably bragged to a friend, who had earlier been a guest at Rose Hill, of his claim to be able to see the church spire. His friend, being fairly familiar with the area, obviously thought he was on to a good thing, took on the wager and was probably invited again to Rose Hill, where the matter would be settled.

Unfortunately for him, Mr Fuller was too smart!

It all sounds very feasible and it would appear to fit John Fuller's post-Parliamentary mood. He would have seen this as a great joke and although it would have cost more to build the Sugar Loaf than he would ever have won on the bet, it probably gave him great satisfaction to see if it could be achieved. Apart from that, it seems too much of a coincidence for such a strange shaped structure to be placed where it is, were there no truth in the tale. It seems 99 per cent certain the story is true in this case, although with John Fuller you can never really be sure!

There is another, less convincing story about the Sugar Loaf. It states that Fuller put up the cone so that people passing through the neighbourhood and viewing it from a distance would believe he had erected a church and consider him a good man for doing so.

Whatever the reasons for its construction, incredibly the structure, which once had two floors, was later used as a dwelling. More light was thrown on this as the result of a chance friendship struck up a few years ago between Sussex farmer, Alan Catt, of East Guldeford, whose family once farmed the area around Brightling, and a Canadian tobacco farmer.

Alan's daughter Jane, who had emigrated to Canada and living in the Woodstock area of Ontario, initiated the friendship when she sent her father a newspaper cutting which told of the remarkable escape from a light aircraft crash of a Mr Lyle Catt. Jane thought that apart from the same name, there were other coincidences between the two families and sent her father the cutting out of interest.

Alan made contact with his Canadian counterpart, wished him a speedy recovery and, although determining they were not related, found there was a most definite connection with the county. Lyle Catt and his wife could trace their origins in England to the Sussex area and had heard many references to the Sugar Loaf from members of their family, who had emigrated to Canada in 1911.

Lyle's grandmother, who died on April 24, 1961, used to talk about 'our home' and said she remembered living in the Sugar Loaf when she was growing up. She was born Mabel Crouch, in July 1879, the daughter of Simon Crouch. Lyle goes on to say that his father, Dennis Catt, was most probably born in the Sugar Loaf on March 21, 1898. The tentacles of the Fuller story are indeed far-reaching!

It is believed the Sugar Loaf was occupied as a dwelling until as late as the 1930s. It contained a living room and bedroom. A bakehouse and scullery were situated in an outbuilding (now gone) which stood close by. To view the Sugar Loaf today, it seems quite amazing to think that people actually lived in such cramped conditions.

In the early 1960s the Sugar Loaf was nearly demolished. Farmer Mr Baker, on whose land the Sugar Loaf stood, thought it too much of a liability and proposed to knock it down if he found no-one to accept it as a gift. The Sussex Archaeological Society turned down the offer saying it was not a historic building. Neither Battle Council nor the County Council were prepared to spend ratepayers' money on the necessary renovation, so a private 'Repair the Sugar Loaf Fund' was started by Major Grissell of Brightling Park. This quickly raised £450, and the structure was renovated over a two-week period in 1961, whereupon the County Council finally agreed to finance its future upkeep.

It is difficult to put a date on the building of the Sugar Loaf, but possibly it was between 1810 and the late 1820s.

The stone spire of
St Giles' Church, Dallington

THE FINAL WORD

Many people consider they are descended from the Fuller family and in certain cases perhaps they are right. However, some make strong insistence that they are directly descended from John Fuller himself, but considering he remained a bachelor, without legitimate issue, it would be a very hard thing to prove!

One of the best known and most curious claims happened in 1915, when a man named Peter Fuller, a mechanic of Tonbridge, declared that he could prove his descent through the Fuller line for 286 years and he wanted his share of the estate.

He drummed up enough local interest and a public meeting was held in order to raise £10,000 to enable him to further his claim through the courts.

He estimated that the Fuller fortune was worth at least £2 million and he stated that as he was a very generous man, he promised that when his claim was proved he would give it all away to the poor.

Sadly for Peter Fuller — and the poor — his claim was found to be riddled with flaws and, despite the support of a London newspaper, the whole matter faded out with no satisfactory conclusion.

As far as John Fuller's descendants and the disposal of Rose Hill are concerned, having no legitimate heir, the house passed to his closest relative, Augustus Elliot Fuller, who served as Member of Parliament for East Sussex from 1841 until his death in 1857. Augustus was a keen huntsman and sportsman and owner of prestigious kennels at Rose Hill, where, it is believed, the famous Sussex spaniel may have been introduced. This unique hunting dog is still bred in the area today by Mrs Anne Findlay at the Oldholbans Kennels, a short distance from Brightling Park.

As well as Rose Hill, Augustus Elliot Fuller held the estates of Catsfield and Hooe, which eventually passed to another of John Fuller's

The Sussex spaniel

nephews, Sir Peregrine Fuller Palmer Acland, who sold them to Thomas Brassey in 1864.

In 1801, Augustus Elliot Fuller married Clara, daughter of Owen Putland Meyrick Esq of Bodorgan, Anglesey in Wales. Their only son, Owen John Augustus, assumed the name of Meyrick in addition to Fuller in 1825 and is best remembered for his involvement in the development of Bournemouth as a seaside resort. He died unmarried in 1876.

In 1879 Sir George Augustus Elliot Tapps-Gervis-Meyrick sold the estate to Percy Tew who renamed the house Brightling Park. He was succeeded by his son, Thomas Percy Tew, who died in 1953.

The property is now owned by the family of Mrs R Grissell, who was first married to the son of Thomas Percy Tew, killed in 1940 during the Second World War.

The follies of John Fuller remain one of the best preserved group of buildings in the country and this is due in no small part to the work of the Sussex Historic Gardens Restoration Society and the East Sussex County Council who have done much fine restoration work. English Heritage have also shown interest by providing funds to repair the Coadestone summerhouse in Brightling Park.

Apart from the follies, another colourful reminder of Jack Fuller can be seen today in the shape of the morris dancers which bear his name. Formed in 1978, Mad Jack's Morris have spread the Fuller story across the country and abroad. An emblem of the Sugar Loaf is incorporated into their colourful outfits and they can be seen regularly around the area in the summer months. Mr Fuller would have been most impressed!

He would also have seen the funny side of the sign hanging outside the village restaurant which bears his name. The wording gets many a puzzled look and prompts much scrambling for a Latin dictionary. Without giving too much away, suffice to say the wording is the result of the imagination of the craftsman who made the sign. Given a free rein, he has created a teaser of which Mr Fuller would have been most proud.

A final word about John Fuller: Thanks to his strange constructions around the village of Brightling, he certainly will not be forgotten that easily and hopefully people will remember him for the many good things he achieved in his eventful life. Was he really mad? Not a bit of it. He was just a child of his times; the colourful, eccentric and never-to-be-repeated times of Georgian England; a larger-than-life character whose greatest wish was to be remembered by future generations. He has succeeded and at the same time kept us guessing.

I hope I have been able to spread a little light on the subject. If and when time travel is ever perfected, my first stop will undoubtedly

Mad Jack's Morris side was formed in 1978. The Sugar Loaf is portrayed on their badge. These enthusiastic dancers have spread the name of Jack Fuller across the country and have made regular visits to the continent. The unique collecting pot (below) gives us another image of Mad Jack and was once regularly used by the side. It is made of fibreglass and resin and the top hat raises to accept donations. It was made by Mr Ken Cox be Brightling in Georgian times. I will step out from my time machine, shake Mr Fuller by the hand and over a bottle of port I will really get to the bottom of all the questions I am unable to answer from this day and age. Until then, thank you John Fuller — for the memories. It has been mostly fun trying to unscramble your secrets. But you are still the winner!

Possibly the best tribute to John Fuller comes from a letter written to the *Sussex County Magazine* of July 1933 by Edward Shoosmith and it provides a fitting close to the story:

'May his soul rest in peace or travel happily over Elysian fields, for in Sussex he was a good man.'

I'll settle for that.

Jack Fuller's, formerly The Fuller's Arms with its eye-catching and puzzling sign

Chronology of events during Fuller's life

1757 Robert Clive's victory wins Bengal and ensures British domination of India
1759 Wolfe defeats French at Quebec
1760 George III comes to throne
1764 James Hargreaves invents Spinning Jenny, which produced yarn faster than wheel
1765 James Watt invents separate condenser, improves efficiency and fuel economy
1767 Canal joins Manchester to Merseyside
1771 Water power used to drive spinning frame. Birth of the cotton mill
1773 Boston Tea Party introduces American War of Independence
1775 British defeated at Bunker's Hill
1776 American colonies declare independence
1781 Captain Cook lands at Botany Bay
1783 William Pitt the Younger becomes Prime Minister at the age of 24
1794 War with France
1798 Irish rising crushed at Vinegar Hill
1799 Combination Acts to prevent growth of trade unions
1800 Act of Union with Ireland. Irish represented at Westminster
1801 Pitt resigns over Catholic Emancipation issue
1802 Peace of Amiens. Brief interlude in fighting with France
1805 Battle of Trafalgar. Nelson killed on HMS Victory
1806 Death of Pitt
1807 Slave trade abolished
1808 Peninsular War begins
1809 Duel between George Canning and Lord Castlereagh over Walcheren Expedition
1811 Appointment of Prince of Wales as Regent
1812 Prime Minister Spencer Perceval assassinated
1815 Napoleon defeated by Duke of Wellington at Waterloo
1820 George IV comes to the throne
1821 Further rejection of Catholic Relief Bill
1825 George Stephenson — Stockton-Darlington railway opened. First steam-hauled public line
1828 Duke of Wellington becomes Prime Minister
1829 Catholic emancipation; Sir Robert Peel establishes Metropolitan Police Force
1830 Low wages/unemployment among farm labourers causes riots; Liverpool-Manchester railway opens; William IV comes to throne
1832 Reform Act passed; Criminal Law Reforms by Peel. Capital punishment abolished for lesser crimes
1833 Keeping of slaves forbidden in British possessions
1834 New Poor Law introduced; Peel becomes Prime Minister; Tolpuddle Martyrs transported; Houses of Parliament burnt down

Acknowledgements

During my research on John Fuller I have travelled to many different parts of the country, met so many helpful people and found myself in many interesting situations. How can I ever forget the day, in the company of Mr Ian Cox, I climbed, heart in mouth, to the top of the Brightling Needle; or the chilly December morning, in the capable hands of Mr Frank Gasson and his son David, when I was accompanied up the tower of Brightling Church to clamber unceremoniously through the dust, seeking out the inscriptions on the bells; or the thrill of lecturing on the subject from the pulpit at Brightling Church and in the process raising money for this wonderful building. So many fine memories. My thanks to those who made them possible.

My thanks to Brian Pennells for initiating my interest in John Fuller over 30 years ago. Yes Brian, you *really* started something!

I wish also to express my sincere gratitude to Mrs Rosemary Grissell, without whose initial help and encouragement nothing would have been published at all.

My thanks to the helpful and friendly staff in all the reference libraries and records offices I have visited or written to for information. I can honestly say I have not had one unfriendly word from any of them. Top of this list must be the wonderful ladies of Battle Library, Liz, Pat, Andrea, Cynthia, Chris and Bridget, who have been absolutely incredible in seeking out books I never knew existed. Thank you. I'll 'trouble' you no more!

My thanks to the staff at the House of Lords Records Office, Royal Institution of Great Britain, East Sussex Records Office, West Sussex Records Office, Hampshire Records Office, Leicestershire Records Office, Eastbourne, Hastings and Bexhill Libraries, Marylebone Records Office, Central London Records Office, Public Records Office, Bodleian Library, Cambridge University Library, British Museum, Eton College, Charterhouse School, Trinity House, The Royal College of Physicians, Freemasons Hall, Boodles Club, The Herschel Museum, Bath, The Royal Institute of Architects, The National Portrait Gallery, Westminster Library, The National Trust.

To Mr Jim Past, the former administrator of Bodiam Castle for his help and hospitality; Messrs H and G Grissell; Mrs Mary Cox; Mr Forvague of Herringtons, solicitors of Battle; Alan Catt; Miss Bessie Russell; Mrs Anne Findlay; Ralfe Whistler; Roger and Shirl Berman of Jack Fuller's; Colin Spray and staff at Dataset; Dave Brown for drawing the map; Keith Fitz Hugh for his patient reading of the text; Marshall Coombs, Nick Lynas and others of Mad Jack's Morris; the owners of Tanners Manor; my working colleague, Alan Jones, whose enthusiasm for the Georgian era matches my own; and to everyone who has helped me in any way in the preparation of this book.

I would also like to acknowledge the work of the Sussex Historic Gardens Restoration Society, the East Sussex County Council and English Heritage in helping to restore the follies of John Fuller. Much fine work has been done at Brightling during the years, so keeping them to the fore as one of the best preserved set of buildings in the country.

But last and certainly not least, I would like to thank Jan Roadnight for all the help and support she has given me in putting the book together. Thank you for keeping me sane?

Picture credits

I would like to thank the following for their kind permission to reproduce illustrations: *Pages* **40, 62/63, 68/69, 70, 74,** Reproduced by courtesy of the Trustees of the British Museum; **18, 90, 88, 89,** The Bodleian Library, Oxford; **98, 114, cover,** By courtesy of The Royal Institution of Great Britain; **45,** The Bowood House Collection, reproduced by permission of The Earl of Shelburne; **102,** The Bank of England; **36/37, 95, 101,** The National Portrait Gallery; **9,** English Heritage; **108/109,** The National Trust; **109,** Mr Jim Past; **112,** Peter Roadnight; **83, 84, 137,** Mr Ralfe Whistler; **58, 60, 111,** East Sussex Records Office; **80,** Mrs Rosemary Grissell; **47,** Tunbridge Wells Museum and Art Gallery; **14, 127, 141,** Brightling Parochial Council; **136,** British Architectural Library, RIBA, London; **104,** Mr Mike Moss, Curator of the Redoubt Fortress, Eastbourne; **147,** Mrs Anne Findlay; **26/27,** Herringtons Solicitors, Battle; **121, 150,** Mr and Mrs Berman; **148/149,** Mad Jack's Morris; **20, inside back cover,** Dave Brown.